MYSTERIES, LEGENDS, AND
UNEXPLAINED PHENOMENA

WEREWOLVES

D1126923

MYSTERIES, LEGENDS, AND UNEXPLAINED PHENOMENA

Astrology and Divination

ESP, Psychokinesis, and Psychics

Ghosts and Haunted Places

UFOs and Aliens

Werewolves

MYSTERIES, LEGENDS, AND UNEXPLAINED PHENOMENA

WEREWOLVES

LINDA S. GODFREY

Consulting Editor: Rosemary Ellen Guiley

Checkmark Books

An imprint of Infobase Publishing

WEREWOLVES

Checkmark Books
An imprint of Infobase Publishing
132 West 31st Street
New York NY 10001

ISBN-13: 978-1-60413-319-6
ISBN-10: 1-6041-3319-8

Library of Congress has cataloged the hardcover edition as follows:

Godfrey, Linda S.
  Werewolves / Linda S. Godfrey.
      p. cm. -- (Mysteries, legends, and unexplained phenomena)
  Includes bibliographical references and index.
  ISBN-13: 978-0-7910-9399-3
  ISBN-10: 0-7910-9399-9
  1. Werewolves. I. Title. II. Series.

  GR830.W4G64 2008
  398.24'54—dc22 2007023044

Checkmark Books are available at special discounts when purchased in bulk quantities for businesses, associations, institutions, or sales promotions. Please call our Special Sales Department in New York at (212) 967-8800 or (800) 322-8755.

You can find Chelsea House on the World Wide Web at http://www.chelseahouse.com

Text design by James Scotto-Lavino
Cover design by Ben Peterson

Printed in the United States of America

Bang FOF 10 9 8 7 6 5 4 3 2 1

This book is printed on acid-free paper.

Contents

Foreword   6

Introduction   11

1   Werewolves: Special Effects or True Live Action?   17

2   WWF, the Worldwide Werewolf Federation   25

3   The Mystery of Werewolf History   31

4   Dude, Where's My Werewolf? The Beast of Bray Road   41

5   Will the Real Werewolf Please Stand Up?   49

6   Werewolves in the Twilight Zone: The Spook Factor   57

7   Did You See What I Saw? Hoax and Illusion   67

8   If It Walks Like a Werewolf...   75

9   Celebrity Were-mania: Howling with the Stars   83

10 Your Field Guide to Werewolves   93

Timeline   103

Glossary   107

Endnotes   110

Further Resources   114

Bibliography   118

Index   121

About the Author   127

About the Consulting Editor   128

Foreword

Did you ever have an experience that turned your whole world upside down? Maybe you saw a ghost or a UFO. Perhaps you had an unusual, vivid dream that seemed real. Maybe you suddenly knew that a certain event was going to happen in the future. Or, perhaps you saw a creature or a being that did not fit the description of anything known in the natural world. At first you might have thought your imagination was playing tricks on you. Then, perhaps, you wondered about what you experienced and went looking for an explanation.

Every day and night people have experiences they can't explain. For many people these events are life changing. Their comfort zone of what they can accept as "real" is put to the test. It takes only one such experience for people to question the reality of the mysterious worlds that might exist beyond the one we live in. Perhaps you haven't encountered the unknown, but you have an intense curiosity about it. Either way, by picking up this book you've started an adventure to explore and learn more, and you've come to the right place! The book you hold has been written by a leading expert in the paranormal–someone who understands unusual experiences and who knows the answers to your questions.

As a seeker of knowledge, you have plenty of company. Mythology, folklore, and records of the past show that human beings have had paranormal experiences throughout history. Even prehistoric cave paintings and gravesites indicate that early humans had concepts of the supernatural and of an afterlife. Humans have always sought to understand paranormal experiences and to put them into a frame of reference that makes sense to us in our daily lives. Some of the greatest minds in history have grappled with questions about the paranormal. For example, Greek philosopher Plato pondered the nature of dreams and how we "travel" during them. Isaac Newton was interested in the esoteric study of alchemy, which has magical elements, and St. Thomas Aquinas explored the nature of angels and spirits. Philosopher William James joined organizations dedicated to psychical research, and even the inventor of the light bulb, Thomas Alva Edison, tried to build a device that could talk to the dead. More recently physicists such as David Bohm, Stephen Hawking, William Tiller, and Michio Kaku have developed ideas that may help explain how and why paranormal phenomena happen, and neuroscience researchers like Michael Persinger have explored the nature of consciousness.

Exactly what is a paranormal experience or phenomenon? "Para" is derived from a Latin term for "beyond." So "paranormal" means "beyond normal," or things that do not fit what we experience through our five senses alone and which do not follow the laws we observe in nature and in science. Paranormal experiences and phenomena run the gamut from the awesome and marvelous, such as angels and miracles, to the downright terrifying, such as vampires and werewolves.

Paranormal experiences have been consistent throughout the ages, but explanations of them have changed as societies, cultures, and technologies have changed. For example, our ancestors were much closer to the invisible realms. In times when life was simpler, they saw, felt, and experienced other realities on a daily basis. When night fell, the darkness was thick and quiet, and it was easier to see unusual things, such as ghosts. They had no electricity to keep the night lit up. They had no media for constant communication and entertainment. Travel was difficult. They had more time to notice subtle things that were just beyond their ordinary senses. Few doubted their experiences. They accepted the invisible realms as an extension of ordinary life.

Today we have many distractions. We are constantly busy from the time we wake up until we go to bed. The world is full of light and noise 24 hours a day, seven days a week. We have television, the

Internet, computer games, and cell phones to keep us busy, busy, busy. We are ruled by technology and science. Yet, we still have paranormal experiences very similar to those of our ancestors. Because these occurrences do not fit neatly into science and technology, many people think they are illusions, and there are plenty of skeptics always ready to debunk the paranormal and reinforce that idea.

In roughly the past 100 years, though, several scientists have studied the paranormal and attempted to find scientific evidence for it. Psychic phenomena have proven difficult to observe and measure according to scientific standards. However, lack of scientific proof does not mean paranormal experiences do not happen. Courageous scientists are still looking for bridges between science and the supernatural.

My personal experiences are behind my lifelong study of the paranormal. Like many children I had invisible playmates when I was very young, and I saw strange lights in the yard and woods that I instinctively knew were the nature spirits who lived there. Children seem to be very open to paranormal phenomena, but their ability to have these experiences often fades away as they become more involved in the outside world, or, perhaps, as adults tell them not to believe in what they experience, that it's only in their imagination. Even when I was very young, I was puzzled that other people would tell me with great authority that I did not experience what I knew I did.

A major reason for my interest in the paranormal is precognitive dreaming experienced by members of my family. Precognition means "fore knowing," or knowing the future. My mother had a lot of psychic experiences, including dreams of future events. As a teen it seemed amazing to me that dreams could show us the future. I was determined to learn more about this and to have such dreams myself. I found books that explained extrasensory perception, the knowing of information beyond the five senses. I learned about dreams and experimented with them. I taught myself to visit distant places in my dreams and to notice details about them that I could later verify in the physical world. I learned how to send people telepathic messages in dreams and how to receive messages in dreams. Every night became an exciting adventure.

Those interests led me to other areas of the paranormal. Pretty soon I was engrossed in studying all kinds of topics. I learned different techniques for divination, including the Tarot. I learned how to meditate. I took courses to develop my own psychic skills, and I gave psychic readings to others. Everyone has at least some natural psychic ability and can improve it with attention and practice.

Next I turned my attention to the skies, to ufology, and what might be "out there" in space. I studied the lore of angels and fairies. I delved into the dark shadowy realm of demons and monsters. I learned the principles of real magic and spell casting. I undertook investigations of haunted places. I learned how to see auras and do energy healing. I even participated in some formal scientific laboratory experiments for telepathy.

My studies led me to have many kinds of experiences that have enriched my understanding of the paranormal. I cannot say that I can prove anything in scientific terms. It may be some time yet before science and the paranormal stop flirting with each other and really get together. Meanwhile, we can still learn a great deal from our personal experiences. At the very least, our paranormal experiences contribute to our inner wisdom. I encourage others to do the same as I do. Look first for natural explanations of strange phenomena. If natural explanations cannot be found or seem unlikely, consider paranormal explanations. Many paranormal experiences fall into a vague area, where although a natural cause might exist, we simply don't know what could explain them. In that case I tell people to trust their intuition that they had a paranormal experience. Sometimes the explanation makes itself known later on.

I have concluded from my studies and experiences that invisible dimensions are layered upon our world, and that many paranormal experiences occur when there are openings between worlds. The doorways often open at unexpected times. You take a trip, visit a haunted place, or have a strange dream–and suddenly reality shifts. You get a glimpse behind the curtain that separates the ordinary from the extraordinary.

The books in this series will introduce you to these exciting and mysterious subjects. You'll learn many things that will astonish you. You'll be given lots of tips for how to explore the paranormal on your own. Paranormal investigation is a popular field, and you don't have to be a scientist or a full-time researcher to explore it. There are many things you can do in your free time. The knowledge you gain from these books will help prepare you for any unusual and unexpected experiences.

As you go deeper into your study of the paranormal, you may come up with new ideas for explanations. That's one of the appealing aspects of paranormal investigation–there is always room for bold ideas. So, keep an open and curious mind, and think big. Mysterious worlds are waiting for you!

—Rosemary Ellen Guiley

Introduction

All over this planet, from the time of the earliest hunter-gatherer societies to the age of cyberspace, people have witnessed mysterious beings that appear to be part wolf and part human: *werewolves*. Owooooo! Their legendary howl has become a pop culture cliché. But you won't see these beasts in your biology textbook or at the local zoo. Their habitats are the moon-dappled forest, the sodden, lonely marsh, and, some would say, the rough edges of the human mind. So, are they real, imaginary, or critters from another dimension? Exactly what is a werewolf?

One expert, Elliott O'Donnell, declared in his 1912 book, *Werewolves*, that there is no one, simple way to define them. As O'Donnell put it, "There are, indeed, so many diverse views…their existence is so keenly disputed, and the subject is capable of being regarded from so many standpoints, that any attempt at definition in a restricted sense would be well-nigh impossible."[1]

There was a time when people dared not even speak the word "werewolf" out loud, for fear the loathsome creature might be lurking near enough to hear its name called and come slashing after its next victim. According to *The Mystic's Menagerie* Web site, merely saying "wolf" in much of Europe during the month of December was once considered bad luck as well as an invitation to the local wolf pack to come and attack livestock or people.[2]

Now, it seems that we hear about and see werewolves everywhere, their images boldly portrayed in every medium. They leap from the pages of comic books and novels and pop howling off the screens of televisions and movie theaters. Some may even thread their pad-footed way into our minds via role-playing or video games. And every Halloween, millions of would-be werewolves in rubber masks and faux-fur tails mingle happily with the populace, barely noticed among costumed witches and cloaked, white-faced vampires.

Ask anyone to describe a werewolf, in fact, and few people will have any problem supplying familiar details. Werewolves are man-sized or bigger, with a full muzzle and oversized, glistening fangs. They run and leap on muscular hind legs, with hand-like paws that end in sharp, raking claws. Werewolves boast pointy ears, glowing eyes, and a full suit of coarse, shaggy fur. Their typical expression is a fierce and challenging glare.

But as common as this furry, fanged image has become in our culture, most people still have little notion of where the idea of werewolves originally came from, or whether it is even possible for such freakish things to exist. It's very easy to shrug them off as nothing more than timeworn myth or, at best, the flea-bitten subject of a few too many "B" horror films.

It isn't as though people of today shun the paranormal entirely. A November 2005 Gallup Poll showed that 38 percent of Americans believe houses may be haunted by ghosts.[3] The same poll revealed that 25 percent of the United States population believes that our lives can be affected by the positions of planets and stars in relation to the Earth. Almost as many agree that extraterrestrial beings have visited Earth and that some people can communicate with the dead. This poll didn't ask whether or not people believed in werewolves, but it's likely that if it had, only a very small percentage would have replied positively. Almost everyone knows someone who claims to have seen a ghost or UFO, after all, but very few people claim to have seen a werewolf.

And yet, there was a time in Medieval Europe when virtually everyone—from uneducated peasants to very learned clergymen, from town magistrates to crown princes—took for granted that such creatures existed. It was also widely believed that werewolves were supernatural in nature, went hand in paw with witchcraft, and were the particular handiwork of the devil. Alleged werewolf encounters occurred by the dozens in some villages, with many livestock raids and savage murders blamed on werewolves by fearful peasants. Many people, most of them probably innocent of wrongdoing, were executed during the years of the bloody witch and werewolf trials in Europe.

Werewolf attacks seemed to continue even after the trials began to lose steam in the 1600s. A typical incident occurred in North Wales in 1790, when an oversized, black animal with a wolfen appearance scared the daylights out of a small community there. The creature attacked a stagecoach, actually managing to knock it over on its side. It then pounced on one of the horses, killing and eating it. The "W" word was invoked immediately.

Adding to the impact of that event, gigantic wolf tracks were discovered in a nearby field within the next year. The tracks led to a bloody, carcass-littered area that had become a killing field for some vicious…and hungry…carnivore. Investigators found the field's owner barricaded inside his house, having narrowly escaped from what he described in Tom Slemen's *The Haunted Liverpool* as "an enormous black animal that resembled a wolf." The wolf not only tore out the throat of the farmer's sheepdog, it battered itself against the wooden door of the farmhouse, walking on two legs to peer into the windows.

According to Slemen, the farmer said its eyes were "blue and seemed intelligent and almost humanlike." Although local men formed a gang and set out in vain pursuit, the creature wound up killing two hapless travelers before its trail of carnage ended.

The strange thing is that in Great Britain, many European countries, and across the U. S. and Canada as well, sightings of a creature that looks suspiciously like a classic werewolf have occurred with alarming frequency in just the past few decades. Does this mean a new day of the wolf is dawning?

Several young people in northwest Michigan think so. In April 2006, three of them—John, Shawn, and Aubrey—witnessed a creature known in local lore as the Dog Man.[4] They had driven out to a long-abandoned schoolhouse south of the little town of Reed City because they had heard rumors that it was haunted. But the thing that appeared to them was no ghost. They saw a man-sized, dark-furred creature with the head and legs of a wolf, standing on two feet and watching them while partially hidden behind a tree. The three were all in their vehicle, and they immediately sped off.

Later, they returned to the scene, drawn by curiosity and the desire to prove to themselves that what they had seen was real. This time, they observed what seemed to be a different creature. It was bigger than the first one, about six inches taller and more muscular, and its fur was gray rather than brown. It approached their car from the rear, sneaking towards them on hind legs until Aubrey, sitting in the back seat, spotted it. In horror, she threw herself backward into the front of the car between the driver's and passenger's seats. The trio again fled the area. Others have confirmed similar experiences in the same place.

But near Oaxaca, Mexico, speeding away may be of no help, since werewolves there may possess cars! In this region, the local people say "La Loba" (Wolf Woman) roams the lonely stretches of desert by moonlight, hunting for the skeletons of dead wolves. She carries them off in her black limo, its windows long shattered from their frames, and knits them into reborn animals who, in turn, become young and lovely wolf maidens.[5]

That story has a ring of pure legend to it, while the Michigan encounters involving specific eyewitness accounts sound more like actual events. But whether these creatures are "real" or not, our fascination with them is undeniable.

Perhaps a few thoughts about the nature of "real" versus "unreal" are necessary here. Is reality only what can be seen or measured with all five senses? Or can a creature only be considered real if it leaves behind footprints or other empirical (measurable) evidence? Some think that the mere act of observing an incident or creature may be enough to pull it into the land of the physical. Physicist Fred Alan Wolf writes in his book *The Eagle's Quest*, "In some sense, each of us 'creates' the reality we see out there from our beliefs."[6]

The line between real and not real can become very tricky, indeed, and may involve everything from advanced physics to personal belief systems. For purposes of this book, those arguments will be left to physicists and theologians in favor of the traditional idea that reality is what people sense around them, and things are either natural or supernatural. Even then, final answers are far from guaranteed.

Some experts have suggested that werewolves are a purely human invention, manufactured to help explain the fact that people have human intellects but animal bodies. From birth, people come hardwired with passions and instincts that can be baffling or even scary, so this "dark" side is blamed on a separate creature. Researcher Kathryn Edwards has noted, "As both human and animal—the one ideally communable and social, the other solitary and fierce—the werewolf embodies the tensions within humanity itself."[7]

But could a mere psychological invention kill a horse or leave a giant footprint in the mud? How could three college students (not to mention hundreds of other witnesses) all see the same creature if it didn't own at least a particle or two of real substance? Shadows do not possess glowing eyes and natural, four-legged wolves do not drive cars in the desert.

This book will prowl through the lore of the manwolf in time and history to find clues to the true nature of the beast. A special side trip will be made to sniff out a huge cluster of modern-day sightings around the United States. Medical case histories of human conditions possibly mistaken for werewolfism will be examined.

Learning from both real-life encounters and the exploration of everything from canine anatomy to Native American lore, a complex picture of the creature begins to emerge. This is not Lon Chaney's werewolf, the familiar version from classic movies. The evidence indicates it is probably something else entirely. Some believe this elusive creature must be hunted down and put under the microscope; others think it should be left alone to work out its own destiny. This book will work toward helping readers form their own opinions.

Finally, it is possible that by investigating something that seems to be half wolf and half human, something may be learned about the wild sides of human nature. Just where does the dividing line between animal and human lie? In this modern day of genetic hybrids and DNA experiments, it is high time to dig for an answer. Do werewolves prowl the highways of the present-day world? When the moon is full, should we expect snarling creatures to come charging at us out of the fog? As the old saying almost goes, where there's smoke, there's bound to be fur.

Werewolves: Special Effects or True Live Action?

Katie Zahn, age 15, and her three friends had a canine creature on their minds the day they drove to Avon Bottoms, a remote wildlife area in southwestern Rock County, Wisconsin. Snuggled in the back seat of their car was a Rottweiler pup that one of the teens had brought along to sell to someone in the area. The teens had arranged to meet the dog's new owners in the wildlife refuge. But after concluding the transaction and saying goodbye to the dog, they decided to explore the area and check out some urban legends they had heard about the swampy, wooded area.

A group of crazy scientists had maintained a secret lab out there, the story went, and had somehow created a human/animal hybrid that escaped into the wilds. The scientists then supposedly abandoned the area in fear and despair, leaving their designer "manimals" on the loose. Every now and then some wide-eyed adventurer reported seeing a canine hybrid still lurking near Avon.

Hoping to spot one of the creatures firsthand, Katie and her friends drove to a field where the creatures had reportedly been seen, but nothing appeared out of the ordinary. The two male teens grabbed their BB guns out of the car trunk and set out to explore while Katie and her girlfriend waited near the car.

It wasn't long before the boys came sprinting back, yelling in terror as they ran for the vehicle. To Katie's great shock, a six-foot tall, fur-covered creature with the head of a wolf was following them. The "wolf" was running on its hind legs. The boys shouted to the girls to get in the car, and Katie and her friend hastily obeyed. One of the boys turned and fired his BB gun at the creature just before scrambling into the car. Either he missed, he would recall later, or the BBs simply bounced off the beast's hide because the creature was not deterred. But no one was interested in staying around to find out why. The driver revved the engine and floored it.

Exciting as the encounter may have been, it wasn't the end of Katie's story. Although the teens were shaken, they finally agreed to drive around a bit longer to see if they could spot the creature again and figure out what it was. They stopped at a bridge and piled out to look down at the river below. There they spied three more of the beasts, very similar to the first one but slightly smaller. They were kneeling by the water and drinking from their hands as humans would. And when they noticed the teens on the bridge observing them, the three wolfish-looking animals stood up on their hind legs as if ready to charge. That scared Katie and her friends into leaving the area permanently. They never went back, and Katie is the only one of the four who will talk publicly about what happened that day.[8]

Was this adventure fact or fiction? Did Katie and her friends really see some kind of wolf/human hybrid? Is it possible they glimpsed a family of true, supernatural werewolves? Or is there actually a canine species unknown to science that has evolved the ability to walk upright? None of these possibilities are easy to accept, accustomed as the modern society is to seeing the world in purely rational ways.

The skeptic might ask whether the whole incident may have been a hoax. Trickery is often suspected when it comes to strange creature sightings, but the idea that four people with matching, Hollywood-movie-quality werewolf suits just happened to be strolling around that secluded nature area, hoping someone would see them and report a false sighting, is almost as hard to swallow as the other possibilities.

Pondering the reality of sightings like Katie Zahn's strikes at the heart of something that has baffled humankind since the dawn of history. Do humans have a closer relationship to wild animals than is generally realized? Are some people able to trade shapes with wolves

Figure 1.1   *An artist's rendering of a typical werewolf.* (Nathan Godfrey)

at will? Is it possible that combination wolf/humans could exist? And if the answer to all these questions is "no," then where do our legends about werewolves and other were-creatures come from?

Many werewolf studies start by hunting for the origins of the word itself. "Werewolf," or, as it used to be spelled, "werwolf," is built upon the Anglo-Saxon word *wer*, meaning "man," plus "wolf." Literally, "manwolf." Another old European spelling of the word, *waer*, connotes something that is evil or has to do with war. In this sense, "werewolf" could mean "evil wolf."[9]

It makes sense, given that in most medieval European lore, a werewolf usually looked just like other wolves except for its large size. But today, the term "werewolf" brings images of tortured Hollywood actors sprouting excess facial fur under a full moon while dodging silver bullets. Of course, in the movies, the werewolf must always bite someone in order to pass the affliction to another victim. But that is mostly modern legend. In the majority of ancient folk tales, it's the werewolf's cousin, the vampire, that reproduces its kind by drinking the blood of some innocent soul. Werewolves usually came into being, according to these older stories, through magic or perhaps from having parents who ran with the pack.

Another name with almost as many ties to Hollywood is "wolf man," used in many motion picture titles. It was especially popular in the early werewolf thrillers from Universal Pictures. In these movies, the monster looked much more human than wolf. Today, "wolf man" is used almost interchangeably with "werewolf" to denote pointy-eared, long-snouted humanoids. But we also use many other monikers for the creature, including **dog man**, **manwolf**,[10] **shape-shifter**, and the Native American skinwalker. Another popular term is lycan or **lycanthrope**, taken from the legendary Greek king, Lycaon. Lycaon earned his fangs by making a forbidden human sacrifice, after which the gods zapped him into wolfen form as punishment. Medically, lycanthrope refers to someone with a mental disorder that makes a person feel they transform physically into a wolf.

Although these terms are meant to describe a creature that combines a wolf or canine body with a human element, each name tells a different story about the nature of the beast. The manwolves

The Dire Wolf: Granddaddy of the Lycans?

Researchers trying to explain sightings of large, strange canine creatures often look to the fossil records in hopes that perhaps a few species thought extinct might not be so very dead, after all. One that is often mentioned is the dire wolf, a wolf-like animal that was once plentiful over the North American continent, and which did possess the massive set of chompers often described on werewolves. But how well does this interesting animal really fit the profile of a wolf man?

One of the biggest problems with that theory is that the dire wolf, or *Canis dirus*, supposedly hasn't been around to bedevil anyone since the Pleistocene era 15,000 years or so ago. And although one song by *The Grateful Dead* rock band describes it as "six hundred pounds of sin,"[11] the dire wolf was in truth only slightly larger than a timber wolf. Many, many skeletons have been found and preserved from California to Florida, with more than 2,000 recovered from California's La Brea tar pits alone.[12]

The dire wolf did have a larger, rounder head than today's wolves, along with shorter, thicker legs. With its big fangs, it would probably not have been pleasant to encounter in a lonely forest. But nothing in its skeletal structure suggests that it could walk upright, even if a few members of its species did somehow miraculously survive into the present. Despite its fearsome appearance, then, the dire wolf is probably just a dead branch of the wolf's family tree. And the only *Canis dirus* likely to be sighted today will be a carefully reconstructed fiberglass sculpture posed in some museum's diorama.

reported by contemporary witnesses like Katie are canine-headed, hairy creatures that zip around on their dog-shaped hind legs, but they are thought by some to be natural animals rather than supernatural beasts. Unlike werewolves from the remote past or medieval times, numerous observers are still spotting these creatures.[13]

Shape-shifters also span ancient and contemporary lore. Usually thought to be the work of **magicians** or **shamans**, they are found in the myths and superstitions of almost every tribal society around the world. These shamans are said to use magic rituals to assume or project the form of certain animals. A skinwalker or skinchanger is a type of shape-shifter acknowledged by many Native Americans. The Navajo call them *yenaldlooshi*, and fear them as malevolent "witches" who usually appear in the shape of a coyote.[14]

This leaves the ongoing argument over whether the creatures that modern-day people continue to glimpse in the forests and cornfields of the United States, Canada, and Europe are indeed entities from another world or just very elusive, flesh-and-blood animals that happen to have learned how to walk upright.

Many leading **cryptozoologists**, or researchers who study "hidden" animals, believe that these beasts are in reality a smaller, differently shaped species of **Bigfoot**, the legendary ape-man reportedly sighted in remote wilderness areas. Other researchers think they are a separate, previously unknown canine species, perhaps some sort of holdover from the last Ice Age when many large and now extinct carnivores walked the land.[15]

Supporting that view, extremely large dog-like footprints have been found at sighting areas in Wisconsin and Georgia, and most witnesses have observed that the creatures obeyed all the laws of physics as any animal would. One or two creatures have left scratches on cars, and many have been observed eating what looks like scavenged animal carcasses. It's hard to imagine any critter from another world wanting to come here simply to satisfy cravings for a bite of mangled roadkill.

Traditional, supernatural werewolves, on the other hand, are usually seen making their own, fresh kills, with a marked preference for human flesh. While they, too, leave footprints and can interact with physical bodies, they are apt to revert back to human form in daylight or when dead. Sometimes they are seen wearing clothing. Their strength is superhuman.

Flesh or fantasy? A real creature to be feared or an ancient nightmare that can safely be forgotten? There are many more arguments to explore on both sides as we attempt to get to the bottom of what Katie saw in Avon Bottoms.

WWF, the Worldwide Werewolf Federation

On the shores of a lake surrounded by woods in the heart of the North American forests, there lived an Ojibwe family—father, mother, two sons, and a daughter—who had left their tribe to avoid having to make war on their neighbors. The father was a man of peace, and even though his family often suffered from hunger and from the lack of social contact, he preferred their solitary life to one of violence.

Eventually, the father grew ill, and knowing he was about to die, he gathered his family to tell them his last wishes. The youngest son was small for his age and sickly. The father made his daughter and oldest son swear to him that they would always care for their younger brother's needs. They agreed, and the father died content.

Six months later, the mother passed on as well, leaving the sister and oldest brother to make good on their promise to watch and provide for the youngest son. They were obedient for a while, but eventually loneliness overtook the oldest son. He craved other young men to hunt with and a young woman to take for a wife. One day he slipped away to a village on another part of the lake and never returned.

The sister did her best to hunt for food and feed herself and the youngest brother, but she also grew lonely. One day, she piled as much wood and food by the tepee as she could manage to put together, told the boy farewell and went off to seek a husband and home of her own.

The little boy was left completely alone, and when he ran out of food, he was forced to scavenge for what he could find in the forest. He began following the packs of wolves that ruled the forest and gobbling down the bits of raw deer, rabbit, and other prey left behind after a kill. Eventually, the wolves accepted him as part of their pack, and the boy came to believe they were his true family.

After some time had passed, the older brother returned to the area on a fishing trip, paddling a canoe with others of his new tribe. He thought he heard someone singing on the shore, and angled in for a closer look. To his surprise, he saw his own little brother, sprouting fur and a tail, turned halfway into a wolf. The boy sang, "My brother, my brother. Ah, see, I am turning into a wolf!"

The older brother was immediately guilt-stricken as he remembered his broken promise to his father, and tried to entice the younger to come back to the village with him. But before the oldest could reach him, the little brother finished changing completely into a wolf. He stared at his faithless sibling for a moment, then howled and ran away into the forest to join the family that had never forsaken him, the wolf pack.

This story was retold from an ancient Ojibwe tale[16] that not only teaches about things like family loyalty and keeping promises, but demonstrates the close ties between humans and their animal "brothers" in many Native American belief systems. In this case, it is not magic but the loyalty and affection between the little brother and his lupine companions that help him make the transition from human to wolf. The story doesn't say if the boy is ever able to change back again, but anyone hearing this tale and then encountering a wolf in the wild might wonder whether this furry creature may have once been human, too.

The idea that humans can become animals and vice versa is common throughout the world. Probably the best-known were-creature from another culture is the French ***loup-garou***, which was usually said to resemble a large, natural wolf. Deciding which wolves were natural and which were transformed humans was not easy, however. Natural wolves ran rampant throughout Europe for much of its history, living on the sheep and livestock they could carry off from small villages as well as the abundant deer and other game in the ancient forests. The main criteria, then, for picking out a werewolf from the ravening pack was usually by its behavior. Particularly large, vicious, and aggressive

Mokwayo, the Wolf Brother, and the Rolling Head

A husband and wife once dwelled alone together in the woods until they had two sons. The older brother was named Wisakedjak, the younger, Mokwayo. They were happy until one day the husband realized his wife was in love with a serpent that lived in the woods. He set out to kill the snake and its family, and then fed his wife their blood. As further punishment, he cut off her head and then ran away to become a star in the sky. The head began to roll across the ground, chasing the two sons, until a crane dropped it into a river. Eventually, the dunked head would become known as the fish called sturgeon.

The older brother had other monsters to slay, and he left Mokwayo to seek his own way. Left to his own devices, Mokwayo turned into a wolf but was killed by water serpents. They committed the further outrage of using Mokwayo's furry skin to cover the door of their lodge. Wisakedjak soon took revenge by slaying their leader, and the serpents fought back by sending a massive flood. Wisakedjak built a raft to survive, and thus brought on the beginning of the time of humans.

—From a widespread Algonquian sacred story, and using the Menominee name of Mokwayo for the wolf brother[17]

wolves, especially if their favorite meat seemed to be human-burger, were immediately suspected.

In countries without wolves, other top-of-the-food-chain carnivores took their place as the were-animal of choice. In Africa, hyenas were often the favored transformational target. From Morocco's Berbers, who believed in nocturnal were-hyenas they called **boudas**,[18] to tribes in the continent's interior who said their witch doctors could shift into hyena form through magic ritual, the people of Africa have long looked warily at this "laughing" scavenger.

On the southern end of Africa, legend has it that there are whole villages full of people able to transform themselves into animals, usually hyenas, at will. They are called the **Chichweya**,[19] and they are believed to conceal animal snouts that grow out of the tops of their heads beneath their sculptural hairdos.

There have been sightings of were-hyenas in the early twentieth century as well. No matter what precautions he took, a British officer, stationed in Nigeria in 1918, was continually frustrated by some animal that ate his livestock. The creature was able to cleanly bite an animal's entire head off. The officer set up a stakeout and shot a big hyena as it ran for a goat the man had set out as bait. He followed the wounded hyena's trail and noticed with astonishment that the hyena prints soon changed into those of a human. Later, he heard that a nearby tribesman had been mysteriously shot to death.[20]

It doesn't seem to matter whether a particular species is reasonably close to human size for it to become a were-creature. In Japan, the petite fox has earned the lion's share of transformation stories despite its relative smallness. In fact, worries about being taken over by a fox spirit were once so common in that country that a temple was established for a god called Mitsumine, where special amulets were sold with the power to ward off were-foxes,[21] which normally transformed from foxes into beautiful women.

Some societies boast creatures that do look and behave suspiciously like the modern-day notion of werewolves. They combine humanlike

Kitsune, the Fox Maiden of Japan

In the forests of Japan, travelers must beware of any beautiful voice crooning sweetly from the undergrowth and beckoning them to stray from the path. The seductive song may be that of a **kitsune**, or fox demon, disguised as a lovely human female. She will try to entice travelers to stay with her, and she may also shear off their hair just for the fun of it. Gluttons, those who overeat, are some of her favorite victims. She also has the ability to shoot fire from her tail, and the fireballs are sometimes seen as lights in marshy areas.

How to protect oneself from a *kitsune*? Many rural areas of Japan are proactive in this matter. Every year, they hold a ritual burning of straw foxes and maidens to ensure that any nearby *kitsune* is held at bay.[23]

Figure 2.1 *The* kitsune, *or Japanese were-fox, lures travelers from their path.* (Nathan Godfrey)

features with animal strength and appearance, and remain an ongoing mystery. In Malaysia, on the southernmost peninsula of Asia, vicious creatures called **santu sakai**, or "mouth men," roam the jungles near Kuala Lumpur. As recently as the late 1960s, two monstrous, fanged creatures chased a hunter there. The beasts attacked the hunter's vehicle, and he only escaped them by using some fancy driving tactics.

Afterward, footprints that looked almost like those of a human, but not quite, were found in the area, along with blood thought to have been shed by the *santu sakai* as they attempted to put their furry fists through the man's windshield![22]

In Timor, an island 400 miles northwest of Australia, certain men are said to have not only the power to change themselves into dogs, but to transform other, unknowing victims into beasts as well. The were-dog arises by night when the shape-shifter's spirit floats away and leaves its human body home in bed. The were-dog then makes its way to a sleeping victim and changes the unfortunate person's **sumangat**, or soul, into a tasty food animal such as a goat. The head of the animal always remains inconveniently human, however, so the were-dog simply lops it off and runs away with the transformed goat body. The next day, looking like his old self again, the were-dog holds a big barbecue without telling anyone where the main course came from.[24]

This global tendency to believe in beast-men (or beast-women) could mean several things. It could be that people everywhere feel some kind of primordial link with the predators of the animal kingdom and build the possibility of creature mergers into their religion and myth in hopes of experiencing that unity. In that case, of course, one man's primordial link is often another man's bizarre nightmare. Another possibility is that animals exist around the world that modern science is not aware of, crouching in whatever wilds are left to them on every continent and finding it increasingly impossible to avoid modern man entirely. Whatever your point of view, once we learn that every society on earth is telling the same old stories about were-creatures, it becomes very hard to put them all down to mere coincidence.

The Mystery of Werewolf History

"I expected them t' burn me alive if ever they caught me. Indeed, they vowed they would do so, at first. I still don't know why they didn't, especially after I told the High Court all the evil I was wont to create. I told them I did kill those children with my bare hands and teeth when the werewolf madness came upon me, and did eat their flesh. That is true. But I also told them it was the Lord of the Forest made me do it, him with the black cloak and the black horse and his kiss as cold as death on my cheek when he took me for his servant.

I was only a lad, no more than eleven, when the witch-boy Pierre brought me to meet that demon in the deep o' the woods. The monster made a mark on our legs with his nail so like a knife, and gave to us each a jar of magical salve and a wolf skin to wear. These turned us into wolves whenever we put them on our bodies. As another sign we were his, he forbade us to cut our left thumbnails, and so these we let grow thick and twisty like the claws of a beast. At least, that is how I tell the tale.

I remember well my kill early in March in the year 1603, when I devoured a little girl named Guyonne who was no more than three years on this earth. There were so many others, although some I just wounded. The fair maid named Marguerite Poirier would have been mine but for her heavy, pointed staff of iron that she jabbed so hard I could not bite her. But it was that servant girl, Jeanne Gaboriaut, who did me in.

She was a pretty lass, and charmed me so that I told her all about my wolf skin, and my hunts for small children, and how I drank the blood of dogs. And then the wench went to the magistrate and called me the loup-garou. She were right, of course. I confessed. But then judges said it weren't right I should be burned at the stake, because my age were so tender and because my bad father beat me. They said I was not ever given proper food, and that I did not have my proper wits about me. So they shut me up in this place, the friary of good Saint Michael the Archangel. If ever I try to leave, they said, they will hang me by the neck from a big oak tree, sure.

So seven long years are passed away and here I sit in this rough prison of a room, all skin and bones because the soup and dark bread they offer does not fill me like the bloody victuals I had when I ran wild. My long, sharp teeth they cannot file short, and my nails still grow sharp like great thorns. But The Lord of the Forest came here twice to try to take me back. He could not because here, I make the sign of the cross and the devil must flee from the consecrated grounds. And in this room, watched by these good Brothers, I, Jean Grenier of Saint-Antoine de Pizon, will remain until Old Man Death finally runs me down and snatches me from this earth. It is more than I deserve according to what I have done to others."

(adapted from The Werewolf in Lore and Legend,
by Montague Summers)[25]

Jean Grenier was a real person who did confess to killing children, and he died in a monastery in 1611 after only eight years of imprisonment. It was never established whether he really did commit cannibalism; small children had gone missing in the region, but Jean was so mentally unstable that people weren't sure whether to believe his confession or not. The mercy granted him by the court was truly

Figure 3.1   *A werewolf attacks a shocked villager.* (Nathan Godfrey)

unusual, since burning had been the standard punishment for witch-craft and werewolfery for centuries.

Although others would still face horrible executions, Jean Grenier's case opened the door for some understanding of the fact that the wretched people usually accused of sorcery often were either mentally ill or likely to have made false confessions during sadistic torture by investigators. By the time the results of Jean Grenier's trial were known, according to author Adam Douglas in *The Beast*

Within, "The age when the courts of France took seriously confessions of diabolical pacts, magic salves and metamorphosing animal pelts had passed forever."[26]

HOWLS FROM THE DISTANT PAST

So how did people get to the point where werewolf trials were necessary in the first place? Many scholars believe that the idea that man and wolf could exchange identities started with Stone Age hunting societies whose members wore wolf skins to ally themselves with the superior hunting abilities of the animal.[27] Eventually, people began to weave man/animal connections into their religions. The very ancient city of Catal Huyuk (cha-tal hooyook) in what is now Asia Minor boasted a bustling population of thousands in 6500 BCE. Wall paintings found by archaeologists in the ruins of Catal Huyuk show priests dressed as vultures. These birds were used to strip corpses clean of flesh, a process called excarnation, so they could be buried neatly under the family's house. Some people think that the birds would have been considered spirit messengers, because they carried away the loved one's body. And it may be that wolves came to serve the same purpose, according to some researchers.[28] Priests of other societies may have dressed as wolves in the same way Catal Huyuk spiritual leaders portrayed the helpful vultures.

We also know that by 3000 BCE, the Egyptians were worshipping animal-headed gods. Anubis, usually shown with the head of a jackal (the closest thing to a wolf in that region), was considered guide to the Underworld. Jackals were scavengers, after all, and would have been observed gnawing at the bones of the dead. It's easy to see how they might have become linked to the afterlife in people's minds.

Animal skins, especially those of bears and wolves, were not connected only with hunters and priests, however. The phrase "going berserk," comes to us from Norse warriors known as "**berserkers**" (or bear-shirts), who often wore entire pelts complete with heads into battle, both to encourage their own ferocity and to strike fear into the enemy. The earliest recorded history of Sweden, written by Snorri Sturluson around 1200 CE, noted these warriors were "mad as hounds or wolves."[29]

Women could also be berserkers. In one Scandinavian tale, the god Thor bragged to a ferryman that he had killed certain berserker women. The ferryman taunted him, saying only a weakling would kill women. Thor, according to Peter Andreas Munch in *Norse Mythology*, replied, "She-wolves, werewolves they were, not real women; they smashed my boat as it lay leaned against the shore; they threatened me with iron bands, and they kneaded Thjalfi (Thor's human companion) like dough."[30] Berserkers who turned into werewolves were known as *vargr.*

In Europe, belief in werewolves and other shape-shifters had become common by the Middle Ages. Of course, werewolves were not the only creatures believed to roam the Continental countryside. "In this supernatural world," says Kathryn A. Edwards in *Werewolves, Witches and Wandering Spirits*, "...ghosts and spirits, werewolves and witches, demons and dwarves all played a role."[31] But from the lands of the Caucasus Mountains to the British Isles, werewolves always seemed to draw special attention.

Skulking lycans also prowled the land of shamrocks and leprechauns, for instance. Historian Montague Summers wrote, "The evidence for werewolfism in Ireland is of immemorial antiquity and persists through the centuries. **Lycanthropy** was for the most part believed to run in families." Summers discussed one man who was named *Faelad*, or "wolf-shapes," because he and his sons shifted into wolf form whenever they felt like feasting on a neighbor's fresh leg of mutton.[32]

Werewolfery could also result from a curse. The legendary St. Patrick, Christian missionary to Ireland in the fifth century CE, was ridiculed by one clan who howled at him like wolves. Folklore has it that as a result, the men from that family were compelled to change into wolves every seven years.

Summers quoted a Bishop Maiolo as saying there were "many werewolves in Russia…haunting above all the Caucasus and Ural Mountains." He also told of the Siberian Yakuts, who believed that

Figure 3.2 *A werewolf, depicted here with wild but humanlike features, raids a farm.* (Mary Evans Picture Library)

The Medieval Witch and Werewolf Trial Craze

Few movements in history have inspired the sheer terror of the centuries-long bloodbath known as the Medieval Inquisition. Specially appointed officials known as Inquisitors roamed every province of Europe, questioning villagers about their neighbors and holding investigations that often ended with the accused person burned at the stake. Often confessions were obtained by tortures such as applying large screws to crush people's thumbs, or by stretching their bodies on racks. Although originally appointed to root out heretics (those who practiced forms of religion other than the state-sponsored version of Christianity), Inquisitors were soon also hunting, torturing, and burning men and women accused of being witches and werewolves, as well. Their official crime? Sorcery.

Ironically, in the eighth century, church leaders and Charlemagne, founder of the Holy Roman Empire, had issued decrees stating that witches did not exist, and that anyone burning a so-called "witch" was subject to the death penalty.[33] Werewolfism was considered part and parcel of witchcraft. But about 700 years later, in 1484, Pope Innocent VIII issued a proclamation that gave power to those already exterminating heretics to wipe out witchcraft as well. Popular zeal for this goal increased two years later when an explosive book called *Malleus Maleficarum* was published. Its name meant "The Witch's Hammer." It not only contained the words of the Pope's decree, it explained and laid out all the collected lore of witchery, shape-shifting, and Satanic rituals that Inquisitors had put together, and demanded that all other authorities join in wiping these devilish practices from the land.

In some areas, entire villages were depopulated. Anyone could be accused, and the flimsiest of evidence was accepted. Older women were the main victims, but eventually the hysteria grew to the point

(continues)

(continued)

where people of any age or sex and even respected tradesmen, elders, and judges were being thrown on the fire. Thankfully, the worst of it was over by 1600. There are no certain numbers for those killed overall, but between 1580 and 1630, nearly 400 people were tried in the duchy of Lorraine alone, and around 100 included charges of shape-shifting, with 36 of those cases involving wolves.[34] Almost 80 percent were convicted, thanks to skilled torturers who extracted false confessions.

their shamans, or holy men, could not only shape-shift, but that they hid their souls within animals for safekeeping, particularly in fierce predators such as bears or wolves.[35]

Greece was filled with werewolf cults that worshipped Zeus and Apollo as late as the mid-1500s. In 1542, a severe outbreak of lycanthropy among citizens in Constantinople forced Solyman II to execute at least 150 of the ravening "beasts" around that city, in order to protect the rest of the populace.

Werewolfism was almost indistinguishable from vampirism in some Eastern European countries. *Voukoudlaks*, or werewolves, were condemned to live in their tombs like vampires, coming out only during the full moon to satisfy their thirst for human blood. In Serbia, any corpse found not to have decayed within a reasonable time was carefully staked through the heart before reburial.[36]

FROM THE OLD WORLD TO THE NEW

Once Christianity became entrenched in Europe after Constantine made it the official religion of the Roman Empire, werewolves, witches, and sorcerers were declared Satanic in origin. The church embarked on a massive witch and werewolf hunt, executing almost anyone deemed suspicious, even for such minor physical aberrations as eyebrows grown too closely together or palms with a bit of hair growth. In just one 100-year period, from the early 1500s to the early 1600s, 30,000 people were accused of being werewolves, or *loup-garou*, in France[37] and usually burned at the stake. Werewolf researcher Montague Summers said that in the 1500s, "...in France especially the rank foul deeds of werewolfery flourished exceedingly."[38]

A century or so later, when European countries began sending ships to the Americas, seamen, explorers, traders, and settlers brought along the legends and beliefs of their homelands. The United States ended up with *loup-garou* tales in old French settlements like Green Bay, Wisconsin and New Orleans, Louisiana, as well as witch trials in Salem, Massachusetts, and **waarwolf**, or werewolf, stories among the German emigrants of Pennsylvania. Some immigrants believed the werewolves were imported from overseas, hidden inside the bodies of those able to shape-shift or stowed away in the holds of great ships. And today superstitious people insist that these same infernal creatures still rove the contemporary world by night.

Dude, Where's My Werewolf?
The Beast of Bray Road

Fog swirled over the cornfields on a dark Halloween night outside the small town of Elkhorn, Wisconsin. High school student Doris Gipson was on the lookout for stray trick-or-treaters as she left her family home on Highway 11 that evening in 1991. On her way to pick up a young relative in town after a party, Doris chose to take Bray Road, a three-mile stretch of country two-lane that was usually quieter than busy Highway 11. As she neared the intersection with Hospital Road in her blue Plymouth Sundance, she felt one of her front tires rise a little as if she had run over something. Fearing she might have hit a cat or a dog, she slowed down, continuing another 50 to 60 feet before coasting to a stop. It was foggy and hard to see anything very far away, so Doris hopped out of her car and took a few steps toward whatever it was she had run over.

About the time she reached the rear of her car, to her shock and horror Doris saw a large creature emerge from the fog. It was running straight for her on two legs. "It was no dog; it was bigger than me," she would later remember thinking. It had a powerful build, a head like a wolf or dog, and was covered in shaggy fur. She could hear its heavy feet thumping the pavement as it ran. She immediately jumped back into her car and hit the gas. But the creature made a leap for her car and left raking scratch marks on the rear of it. Doris managed to escape into town, but she later drove home via the same route and managed to catch another glimpse of the creature slinking off into the misty night.

Doris told a few of her classmates at Elkhorn Area High School what she had seen, and a school bus driver overheard her and realized that her own daughter, Lori, had witnessed the same creature a few years earlier as she drove home one night from her waitress job in Elkhorn. It turned out that other area residents had seen the beast, too. They all described it as about six feet tall, covered with wild-looking, dark brown fur, with the head of a wolf or German shepherd and glaring yellow eyes that seemed to challenge the observer. Some saw it on four legs, some on two. In several cases it was observed eating roadkill or deer.

Lori and Doris, along with a few others, contacted the Walworth County Animal Control Officer, hoping he could provide an explanation for what they had seen. He could not, but he filed their reports in a manila file folder marked "werewolf." That was what people had started calling the creature, since a werewolf was exactly what it looked like. The school bus driver, in the meantime, had called this author, since I was working as a reporter for a Walworth County newspaper at the time. The newspaper editor and I quickly decided that a county official with a file folder labeled "werewolf" was newsworthy, and I wrote a story about the creature that I dubbed "The Beast of Bray Road." [39]

The story was eventually picked up by Associated Press and received a huge amount of publicity. Busloads of tourists from Illinois came to view Bray Road in hopes of seeing a werewolf, merchants sold werewolf cookies and T-shirts, and a local politician running for office claimed that the werewolf endorsed him. People who lived on Bray Road became very tired of wannabe werewolf hunters shining flashlights in their windows and trespassing on their land in camouflage fatigues, and they began reporting the nighttime stalkers to police.

The media feeding frenzy continued. But the strangest part was that not just reporters and TV shows were calling; many other people who had had their own experiences were also phoning to report sightings. It became evident that this was no isolated cluster of incidents, easily explained away as a "deformed coyote," which was the local

Figure 4.1 *Werewolves, like the one depicted here snacking on an unlucky raccoon, are often sighted at roadside.* (Linda S. Godfrey)

sheriff's favorite explanation. The earliest sighting was in 1936 in nearby Jefferson County, and the incidents ranged southward over the Illinois border and as far east as Milwaukee. Even a radio disc jockey at WTCM in Traverse City, Michigan, phoned to say they had a similar creature there known as the Michigan Dog Man, based on old logging-camp tales.

Stories continued to trickle in over the next 10 years. Many television shows visited Elkhorn to film documentaries about The Beast of Bray Road, and one Hollywood producer tried unsuccessfully to get a movie made. (A group called The Asylum released a mostly unrelated movie with the title *The Beast of Bray Road* to video in 2006.) In 2003, the book *The Beast of Bray Road: Tailing Wisconsin's Werewolf*, was released, and the resulting publicity brought a flurry of new sightings reports.

Many of the reports were about events that had occurred years earlier, but the witnesses had often been too afraid to tell anyone, believing that they were the only people in the world who had seen an actual werewolf. But reading reports from other witnesses made them feel they could finally come forward, many of them said. And they were not all from Wisconsin. Two brothers from the northern tip of New York, near Lake Champlain, wrote to say that they spied two of the wolf-headed creatures running alongside a highway, loping along on two feet. A funeral director from Southern Georgia encountered one in a swamp while hunting arrowheads. Appearing enraged at being spotted, a six-foot manwolf charged at him as if it wanted to attack. The man was able to leave the scene in his truck, but when he went back the next day, he found footprints shaped like a wolf's but as big as a man's size-11 shoe! Reports also came in from around southeastern Wisconsin, northern Wisconsin, from everywhere, in fact, except Bray Road. The creature appeared to have been scared off that road by all the publicity and has only been reported in that vicinity once since the early 1990s.[40]

The Beast may have some friends, too. A smaller number of people have reported seeing what looks exactly like a slightly shorter Bigfoot.

There are big differences between the two creatures. The Beast, or manwolf, has a head like a wolf or German shepherd, with tall, pointy ears on top of its head and a long muzzle. Its hair is shaggy but not flowing. It is sometimes observed to have a tail, and its legs are configured like a canine's. It leaves dog-like prints. The Bigfoot creature does not have visible ears, its hair flows onto its neck like a cape, and the movement of its legs when it walks resembles that of a human's. Its footprints are flat and humanlike.

Still, some people believe that the Beast of Bray Road is actually a small Bigfoot. Other people think it's a hoax. It's true that two farm boys who lived on the road had some fun scaring people with Halloween masks, and that one transient farmer once wore a gorilla suit to scare some teenagers out of parking on his land. (This incident is explored in Chapter 7.) But neither of those events could account for all the sightings over all those years and in other places.

Some believe that the creature has never been caught because it lives in a spirit world part of the time. Southeastern Wisconsin is unique in having many effigy mounds built by ancient Native Americans and shaped like a variety of animals. Could the Beast of Bray Road be an ancient spirit guardian left behind by those people to guard their sacred mounds? Or is the manwolf some kind of supernatural being conjured up by modern day shamans or magicians? Interestingly, there has been no documented case of a human actually being injured by this creature, which is consistent with the theory of a spirit being.

Others would argue that the Beast of Bray Road is an actual, unknown creature, possibly leftover from the past when giant animals, or **megafauna**, roamed this continent. It would have had to hide itself cleverly from man, perhaps living in underground caves and tunnels, and would need to be very intelligent to adapt to changing conditions of climate and food sources. The Beast of Bray Road has been clever enough to keep from being caught or shot so far, despite all the people who have been trying for the past decade and more. In the meantime, the sightings continue.[43]

The Animal Effigy Mounds: Where Manwolves Roam

Thousands of earthen mounds shaped like bears, deer, thunderbirds, turtles, men, and the mysterious water panther once covered much of the southern half of Wisconsin. The mounds, usually located near waterways, were so ancient that the Native tribes first encountered by settlers said they didn't know who made them. Present dating methods estimate that the mounds were built between 800 BCE and 1200 CE.[41] But the Ojibwe, Potawatomi, and Ho-Chunk people all felt that the mounds were sacred and took great care not to disturb them.

The settlers who pushed into the state to farm or log the land were not so sensitive, and many of the mounds were destroyed. In fact, a popular Sunday afternoon activity in the early part of the twentieth century was to hold a "mound dig party" in hopes of finding buried artifacts. But enough of the mounds have been preserved that after much study by

Figure 4.2 *Effigy mounds depicting (clockwise) a deer, a water panther, a dog, and a bird.* (Linda S. Godfrey)

Figure 4.3   *The Beast of Bray Road was sighted in a region that is also home to Indian burial mounds like the Great Bear Indian mound seen here.* (Tom Bean/Corbis)

archaeologists and anthropologists, some interesting things are known about them.

Some, but not all, of the mounds were used for burials. Sheboygan's Indian Mounds Park contains a mound that was opened and found to contain a burial. The remains were recreated by casting them in resin, and replaced into the site with a Plexiglas cover so that the mound can be viewed as it looked when it was opened.

Tribal anthropologists have noted that the mound shapes represent the same totem animals revered by the Ho-Chunk, and many experts think that the far distant ancestors of the Ho-Chunk may have been the

(continues)

(continued)

builders of the effigy mounds. Most agree that the mounds represented important religious beliefs of the builders, and perhaps were intended to harmonize spirits of the sky (birds) with spirits of the water (turtles, lizards, and water panthers) and of the earth (bear, deer).[42] Strangely, a few of the mounds that are shaped like men feature projections on the head that could have represented horns worn by medicine men—or were they meant to show the pointed ears of a wolf-headed, bipedal creature? The true purpose of the animal effigy mounds may never be known, but it is an interesting coincidence that they are found almost nowhere else in the world but the southern half of Wisconsin, which also happens to be the main location of present-day sightings of manwolves.

5

Will the Real Werewolf
Please Stand Up?

Wolves once flourished in India as they did in other wild places around the globe. Adaptive species that they are, wolves often make their dens in unexpected places—even in the giant, conical mounds left by termite colonies in India. So it didn't strike two men as terribly unusual when they discovered several wolves running from a massive cone of dirt in the wilds southwest of Calcutta one day around 1920. What shocked them was the fact that two small human females, about three years and five years old, also came crawling out, and appeared to have been living inside the earthen shelter with the wolves!

The girls did not want to be "rescued," reported the men. Growling, biting, and kicking savagely, they acted like tiny werewolves. One of the men, a missionary named Reverend Singh, took them back to the small orphanage he ran. After seeing to it that they were bathed and cleaned up, he set about trying to teach them proper human behavior. He named the younger Amala, and her supposed older sister, Kamala. It may have occurred to him that publicity about two wild wolf-girls could benefit his orphanage financially.

He soon found, however, that although he had succeeded in taking the girls out of the wolf den, it wasn't so easy to take the wolf den out of the girls. They refused to eat anything but raw meat, ran around on all fours, and would only try to stand up if Singh held meat above them in the same way dogs are taught to beg. They had no interest in human company but loved a hyena cub that was brought for them to play with. They stubbornly refused to be housebroken, urinating and defecating where and when they pleased.

Their behavior continued to dismay everyone who observed them. One of the girls, on finding a dead cow near the compound, attacked the carcass with her hands and teeth, and then secretly dragged parts of it back to the orphanage garden where she could chew on it all she liked. Singh wrote that in the dark, the eyes of both girls glowed a strange, faint blue color. (Many researchers have accused him of making this up, since human eyes lack the necessary membrane to reflect light like those of animals.) The girls also howled plaintively at regular intervals and resisted learning the simplest words.

Amala died of a kidney infection only a year after being taken from the termite mound. Kamala lived eight years after that, until 1929. She had finally managed to learn a few words and even form short sentences. She had acquired toileting skills, as well, and was allowed to go to church services. Sadly, Kamala also fell ill from a kidney infection and died on November 14.

Amala and Kamala were not the only Indian children said to be raised by wolves. A "wolf-boy" was found in Sikandra in 1867 and another near Allahabad in 1926. These feral or "wild" children follow in the tradition of the mythical "Romulus and Remus," legendary founders of Rome who were said to have been suckled by a she-wolf. Actual evidence that any mother wolf nursed and took care of foundling human infants is sadly lacking. Animal expert Lois Bueler states in *Wild Dogs of the World*, "…since wolves nurse their pups for less than two months and subsequently feed them regurgitated food, it would be impossible for a human infant to survive this way."[44]

Still, it's fascinating to contemplate just how a person would turn out if reared by wolves, and with no human parents, church, school, television, or other influences most people take for granted. But could such a crude upbringing turn a human being into a werewolf?

It's true that stories often emphasize the **feral children**'s preference for carrion and raw meat, something that is also believed true of werewolves, and that their nails and hair may be long and claw-like due to lack of grooming. But not even the most enthusiastic supporters of Amala and Kamala ever hinted that the girls grew fangs, pointed ears, body fur, or other hallmarks of werewolves. They were still completely human. They were simply very poorly socialized humans. One researcher, Bruno Bettelheim, went so far as to claim that Amala and Kamala were actually suffering from the childhood mental disorder known as autism,[45] which often results in poor interpersonal skills and what seems like anti-social behavior.

But even if true feral children have actually existed, it is still very unlikely anyone would ever mistake one of them for a wolf or werewolf. Reverend Singh knew immediately on the day he found them in that termite mound that he was looking at small, human females, not little she-wolves, no matter how caked with dirt or contorted their arms and legs might have been. It isn't likely, then, that feral children can be used to explain away the idea of werewolves.

THE ULTIMATE BAD HAIR DAY

There are people with another very rare condition that makes them very hairy who have been credited with inspiring the idea of man-wolves. Individuals born with a trait known as **congenital hypertrichosis** may grow thick, furry hair over more than 90 percent of their bodies, including their faces. A Mexican family with the surname of Ramos-Gomez is famous for this characteristic. Some family members have more hair than others, but a few are almost completely covered with dark fur. Ramos-Gomez sons Victor and Gabriel bill themselves as the "Wolf Brothers," and have traveled the world as a hirsute trapeze act. There is also a young man in China, Yu Zhenhuan, who calls himself "Hairboy" and is 96 percent hairy. A musician, he dreams of becoming the world's first furry rock star.

Figure 5.1 *Hair covers 96 percent of Yu Zhenhuan's body, making him China's hairiest man.* (Claro Cortes IV/Reuters/Corbis)

These people are not werewolves. They are ordinary human beings in every other way, and do not feel compelled to howl at the moon or go prowling for human flesh. They do not have muzzles, fangs, or tails. And given a close, full-body shave, some laser hair removal, or a good waxing, they would not appear wolf-like at all.

Some skeptics have suggested a disease called **porphyria** might be responsible for legends of werewolves. Porphyria is another congenital condition that causes extreme sensitivity to light, tooth and skin discoloration, and sometimes malformation of bones and cartilage. Porphyria can even bring on hypertrichosis. Other symptoms are mental delusions and hysteria. People with extreme forms of this disease, left untreated, might act in strange ways and look abnormal. But again, the condition would not cause anyone to be mistaken for a wolf without a huge amount of imagination on the part of the observer.

LYCANTHROPY: MAD FOR THE MOON?

People who believe that they actually turn into wolves at the full moon often call themselves lycanthropes or lycans, after the Greek king, Lycaon, discussed in Chapter 1. Lycanthropy is also the name psychologists give to a certain mental disorder. It is sometimes called "wolves' fury" and can include symptoms such as howling, skulking around cemeteries, and craving raw meat or carrion. Psychologists say that no matter how much a person with lycanthropy may howl, bite, crawl, or try to scratch fleas from his ears, the feeling of possessing a wolf's body is only a delusion.

According to Rosemary Ellen Guiley in *The Encyclopedia of Vampires, Werewolves, and Other Monsters*, lycanthropy is linked to a host of mental conditions, including schizophrenia, multiple personality disorder, bipolar disorder, drug abuse, clinical vampirism, mental retardation, necrophilia, and other psychological disorders.[46] On top of all that, someone diagnosed with lycanthropy might feel very alienated from society, be obsessed with anything considered "demonic," and even feel a thirst for blood, says Guiley. But, she adds, it has been noted as a mental disease since 130 CE when a Greek doctor Galen first described it.[47]

For those who see all that changing of the physical body as too much trouble, there is another version of lycanthropy

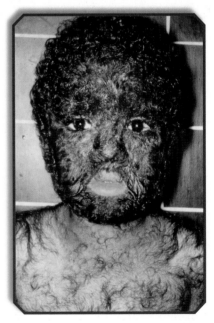

Figure 5.2 *The condition seen here is called hypertrichosis, a genetic disorder that causes excessive hairiness.* (AP)

called **therianthropy**. People in this camp may call themselves therians, for short. They claim to transform only spiritually, while their bodies remain human. Therianthropy may or may not be associated with psychological disorders; those who call themselves therians encompass a wide range of beliefs and practices, from mere fantasizing to costumed role-playing of animal behavior in outdoor settings. Therianthropy may also refer to shape-shifting into animals other than wolves.

Ergot Mania!

The year 1951 was remarkable in many ways. In the United States, the United Nations opened for business in New York City. It was the first year people could buy color TVs or frozen turkey potpies. And in France, in a small village named Pont-Saint-Esprit, it was the year the villagers went mad.

Young girls in white nightgowns, confined to their beds from a strange fever and delirium, began screaming that their bodies were growing bright red flowers. Grown men complained that their heads were no longer made of flesh but lead that had been heated to the melting point, ready to flow over their feather pillows. Children tried to murder their parents with their bare hands. People saw visions of terrible things like skulls that grinned and leered through vacant eye sockets and packs of ravening tigers. In all, 300 people fell victim to a bewildering array of psychotic delusions.

The epidemic might not have been so damaging if people had stayed in their beds, but the mysterious disease made people want to prance about town or jump off buildings as if they were Superman. Some even showed signs of superhuman strength. A handful died, their cardiovascular systems destroyed. After several weeks, police finally traced the

As an explanation for sightings of upright, hairy creatures or fierce wolves with ferocious appetites for human flesh, however, lycanthropy and therianthropy fall short for the same reasons as do feral children and folks with hypertrichosis. The afflicted people are still people, and always recognized as such. It's just very hard to mistake any human for a wolf.

There is another route to believing one's self to have turned into a wolf or other predator without actually sprouting fuzz. Around the

disease to bread baked by a shop whose flour had been contaminated by **ergot**, a fungus that grows on damp grain. Ergot is a storehouse of potent chemicals, and in fact, is the source of the powerful hallucinogen known as LSD.

Ergot poisoning was not new to the area. It ran rampant throughout much of Europe in the cold, damp years from 1250 and 1750,[48] causing much death and disease among poor people who ate mostly rye bread. Historians have also blamed it for the weird behavior that led many to be accused of witchcraft and werewolfism during the medieval witch trials. But this French nightmare in 1951 showed that modern people are not immune from the illness so terrible it was once called "St. Anthony's Fire."

Figure 5.3 *The ergot fungus grows on grain and is a powerful hallucinogen. When eaten by humans it can cause symptoms that resemble the characteristics of a werewolf.* (Linda S. Godfrey)

world, highly trained shamans or tribal spiritual practitioners have claimed that the "inner predator" may be experienced by ingesting certain drugs, mushrooms, or other hallucinogenic substances that can induce trance states. These substances are often dangerous to physical and/or mental health, but subjects claim their experiences feel very real. There is also a substance called ergot, which is a fungus found on rotting cereals such as rye, that may be eaten accidentally, often with disastrous results (see sidebar).

In sixteenth-century Europe, one book of alchemy and magic, *Magiae Naturalis* (Natural Magic) by Giambattista della Porta, gave instructions on which herbs to use in order to bring on hallucinations of shape-shifting power. The potion started with a cup of wine, into which was mixed such dangerous substances as belladonna, or deadly nightshade, mandrake, and henbane. Some very toxic ingredients were also combined to make the "magical salves" that many medieval would-be werewolves applied to their bodies to make themselves transform. Hemlock, bat's blood, and soot were just a few.[49]

In short, if this were a TV game show and we asked the real were-wolf—feral child, lycanthrope, hairy guy, or ergot eater—to stand up, none of them would be able to truthfully rise. For most of them, any alleged werewolfism exists mostly in their heads—or in the case of the Ramos-Gomez brothers, in their epidermis. While there may have been cases where impressionable people have mistaken people with hypertrichosis or ergot convulsions for werewolves, these conditions could only account for a very small fraction of sightings worldwide.

Werewolves in the Twilight Zone: The Spook Factor

Two young sisters, aged seven and 10, were playing in the backyard of their family farm in northern Wisconsin without a thought toward any world beyond their own. Suddenly, they looked up in alarm to discover some sort of wild, hairy beast approaching. In front of them stretched an open field surrounded by woods and separated by a lane with an electric fence on either side. The beast stood in the lane, staring, only a short distance away from the startled sisters. It appeared to be a dark, menacing wolf.

Before the girls could scream or run away, the wolf turned and walked right through the electric fence! The girls continued to watch, afraid but fascinated, as the wolf kept walking toward the woods and then suddenly changed form into a bear! Finally, before reaching the trees, it disappeared into thin air.

REALITY BITES?

The girls' father reported this story, because even several years after the incident occurred, the girls, who still insisted that it really happened, refused to talk to anyone outside their family about it. Both sisters saw the same thing, so it could not have been a hallucination. They may have made it up, but their father doesn't think that's likely. He believes they would eventually have admitted they were playing a trick, had that been the case. They had nothing to gain by lying, and they were not known for inventing strange tales. Their parents absolutely believed that their daughters saw a bear/wolf shape-shifter.[50] And there are many people who insist that's exactly what werewolves are: shape-shifters. If this is true, does it mean that werewolves aren't "real"? As discussed earlier, the nature of reality may be elusive as any unknown creature. But the fact that two witnesses saw the same creature and sequence of events makes it unlikely this was a hallucination.

Of course, physical proof is always desirable. Would the creature be considered real if it had bounced back off the wire fence and left behind footprints or some other kind of evidence? It's possible that even this would not be enough to convince a skeptic that the girls' story is true. But stories of animals with supernatural properties are basic to every culture. And what these girls saw is very similar to some well-known Native American traditions.

SHIFTY CHARACTERS

The idea that werewolves are not natural animals but denizens of a spirit world or, perhaps, another dimension, is common among the indigenous people of North America. They believe that men sometimes have the power to transform, or shift, their human shape into the form of some other creature, and that sometimes animals can shift into human form, as well. Magic rituals, fasting, eating certain psychotropic plants, and highly disciplined spiritual training are all methods used by shamans to enable shape-shifting. But the process is not necessarily limited to medicine men.

David Walks-As-Bear, a Shawnee Nation member who has worked most of his life as a game warden in Michigan, wrote in a column posted on his Web site, http://www.walks-as-bear.com, "For Indians, shape shifting is applied in hunting, song and dance, healing and warfare. A brave will study his spirit animal for many years to learn all of its uniqueness and mannerisms, trying to become one with it or—just like it." He believes that some of the famous Cheyenne Dog Soldiers, elite fighting force of the Cheyenne Nation in the mid-1800s, may actually have been shape-shifters.

"The Cheyenne Dog Men," says Walks-As-Bear, "supposedly were wiped out by the U.S. Army. But there are stories, carried over from the elders that tell of some of the Dog Men actually shape-shifting into the 'real dogs' that they mimicked in battle. Thus, these few escaped the U.S. Army's planned killing of them all back in the 'Battle of Summit Springs' in Colorado."[51] Walks-as-Bear thinks that it's possible the Michigan Dog Men might be a remnant population of some of these forever-changed dog soldiers.

INSTANT MESSAGING, ANIMAL-TO-HUMAN

The idea that the spirits of men and animals can migrate from one host to another is called **metempsychosis**. In an 1871 *Atlantic Monthly* article that attempted to find some historical reason for the idea of werewolves, writer John Fiske described metempsychosis as a belief in the "close community of nature…between man and brute."[52] In this type of belief system, it would be logical to assume that the shape or form of an animal would follow its spirit into a human host. But as with most things in the paranormal realm, hard evidence in support of this theory is scant. In lieu of actual bodies to study, researchers must look for clues in the reports of those who have seen the creatures. Claims coming from such stories, or anecdotes, are known as **anecdotal evidence**.

One anecdotal claim involves **telepathy**, or the trading of thoughts between one mind to another. A number of witnesses have insisted that the beasts they encountered communicated telepathically with them. In *Hunting the American Werewolf*, Renee Fritz reports of chancing upon a wolf-headed creature as she drove to work very early one morning in October 2004, near Sharon, Wisconsin. She felt that the strange being "told" her via mental impressions that if she revealed her sighting to anyone, it would find her and "get her."[53] She was so frightened by this that it took her three days to work up the courage to tell her husband. Thankfully, it seemed to be an empty threat. The creature left her alone.

The idea that an animal or supernatural being could project a telepathic message to a human may seem far-fetched. Yet, many flesh-and-blood human beings claim telepathic abilities, and scientists have investigated them, though without obtaining any conclusive evidence. So if there is such a creature as a wolf or dog that walks upright, who's to say that it couldn't be a bit psychic as well?

HELLHOUNDS AND PHANTOM WOLVES

Wolfmen and giant hounds that vanish and appear are a different matter. British folklore abounds in stories of "hellhounds" and black dogs that are often seen as guardians of the dead. The very earliest hellhound legends are probably related to observations of dogs, wolves, and other canines scavenging burial grounds. An early example is the Greek "Hound of Hell" named Cerberus. Cerberus is described in mythology as a humongous dog with multiple heads (usually three). He guards the gates of Hades to prevent anyone from escaping. Author J.K. Rowling borrowed Cerberus in *Harry Potter and the Sorcerer's Stone* to serve as the three-headed guard dog named "Fluffy."

In Norse mythology, the guardian of the gate to hell is a huge, bloody wolf-dog hybrid named Garm. On the day the world ends, known as Ragnarok, Garm will break free of his chains and leave the entrance to the underworld wide open.[54]

In southern Germany, one of the areas most obsessed with hunting and killing alleged werewolves in medieval times, churches used to keep "miracle books" in which parishioners could record extraordinary occurrences or answers to prayer. Not all the entries were made in a spirit of thankfulness. One woman used the miracle book at the shrine of Saint Anastasia to report that a phantom black dog bedeviled her. Church authorities assumed the hound to be Satan. In the same area of Benedictbeuern, a headless, upright wolf shocked a shepherd out of his mind when it suddenly appeared amid his sheep.[55]

Hunting the American Werewolf includes several modern instances of phantom dogs. One is the story of a Wisconsin man who was terrified to find an upright creature with a "jet black, muscular body" and a face that "looked just like a werewolf" standing outside his bathroom door one morning. When he reached for a baseball bat for defense, the slightly transparent creature vanished.[56]

In the same book, six teenagers exploring the abandoned lake cottage of a supposed witch emerged only to find themselves threatened by the looming shape of an upright wolf materializing out of the darkness. They ran for their lives but, to their relief, the phantom wolf did not follow.[57]

It is impossible to say where these mythological and phantom versions of wolves and dogs come from. The human imagination is one possible source, but legends and stories claim there is a spirit realm from which these beings cross over. Sometimes, the creatures bring a friend or two along for the visit.

CREATURE PARTY TIME

Strange occurrences, it seems, seldom happen in isolation from one another. Prominent paranormal investigators such as long-time researcher and author John Keel have noted that where one odd thing rears its shocking head, others are bound to follow. He calls these places with repeated odd occurrences "window" areas.[58]

In one area of Texas, people have reported seeing Bigfoot, black panthers, unexplained lights, and other strange things around the Big Thicket National Preserve. Black "panthers," sometimes termed "mystery cats," have also been reported in Wisconsin and Michigan near sightings of manwolves. Both states are also rife with sightings of unidentifiable lights, such as the famed Paulding Light on the far western side of Michigan's Upper Peninsula. Explanations for this light phenomenon range from marsh gas to the reflections of auto headlamps on a far-away hill, but witnesses tell of being followed or chased by the lights at close range, or experiencing electronic difficulties with their vehicles as the lights passed through them. Robb Riggs, in *In the Big Thicket: On the Trail of the Wild Man*, wrote "The association of mysterious light-form producing energies and ape-like creature sightings is reported again and again by independent researchers."[59]

By "ape-like," Riggs probably means Bigfoot or Sasquatch, often referred to in southern states as the Skunk Ape. But many times, witnesses

Figure 6.1 *Some werewolf sightings have been connected to UFO encounters, suggesting a possible otherworldly origin for these creatures.* (Linda S. Godfrey)

Figure 6.2 *A frame from the famous Bigfoot film, obtained by Roger Patterson at Bluff Creek in northern California on October 20, 1967. Some believe that the film is a hoax, but no solid proof has been shown either way.* (Fortean Picture Library)

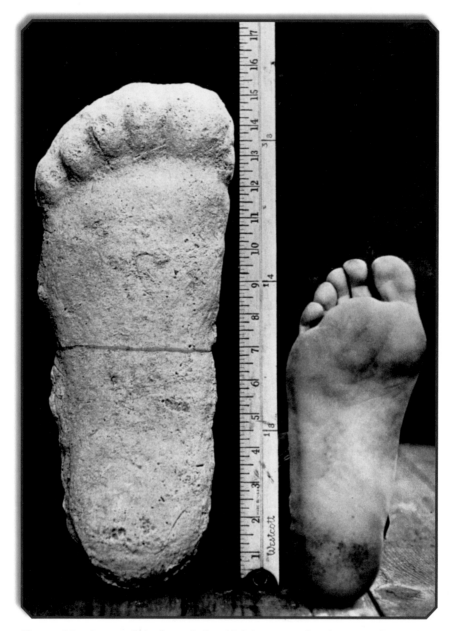

Figure 6.3 *A normal-sized man's foot (right) compared with a cast of a Bigfoot footprint. It is one of several found at Bluff Creek, California, in 1967 after the filming of Bigfoot by Roger Patterson.* (Fortean Picture Library)

assume that any upright, hairy hominid must be a Bigfoot, even if it boasts a dog-like head, body, and legs. It is possible that at least some reported Bigfoot sightings could actually have been upright canines, or manwolves. And vice versa. Strangely, most of the places where manwolves have been seen also host scores of Bigfoot sightings.

One Bigfoot investigator in Texas, Richard Van Dyke of the American Anthropological Research Foundation, differentiated between the two types of creatures in an interview with the author by referring to the wolf-like, upright creatures by their local name of "Snout-Nose." But whatever names are applied to them, it appears that upright, hairy hominids hang together, co-existing in the same habitat, and where one is seen, another is likely to show up.

The idea of different types of hairy, upright creatures sharing similar habitats makes sense. They are likely to share the same needs for water, game, and cover. That does not explain why strange lights and black panthers also pop up in the same area. One theory suggests that all these phenomena are just different forms of a strange trick played on human minds by the electromagnetic properties of certain rock formations. Parts of the human brain can be affected by electromagnetic waves, therefore exposure to these areas can result in hallucinations of certain basic images such as lights or animal forms.

Author Paul Devereux, who has investigated ancient "holy sites" in Europe and North America, discovered that these places often contained large amounts of "magnetic" rock that would cause a compass needle to swing wildly. "There is experimental evidence to show that the human brain is susceptible to quite small changes in the ambient magnetic field," wrote Devereux in his book, *Haunted Land*, "and that this can trigger sensations that are commonly considered as being visionary or paranormal."[60]

In that case, all of these mysterious creatures and phenomena could just be figments of our fertile minds, jiggled into existence by a few zaps from the right kind of rock. But not every sighting of strange phenomena occurs near magnetized rock strata. A very complete geo-

graphical survey would be needed to prove this theory in every location on earth where strange things have been seen.

Perhaps rocks have nothing to do with strange creatures. Another
possible explanation holds that Bigfoot, werewolves, black panthers,
and odd lights (including swamp lights or will-o-the-wisps and UFOs)
are all manifestations of a shape-shifting earth or nature spirit that
shows up in whatever form best suits its purposes. In Scotland, such
spirits are called Kelpies, and often present themselves as a horse or
beautiful maiden in order to lure people into a lake or river where they
are drowned.

Whether it originates from the human body and mind or from
someplace in the "spirit world," the shape-shifter neatly ties together both the phenomenon of disappearing creatures and the
variety of strange things associated with them. Unfortunately, no
scientific method has yet been devised to prove the existence of
shape-shifters. It's up to each individual researcher to decide just
how much weight to give any pile of anecdotal evidence. Many will
keep searching for physical, empirical proof that these creatures
really walk among us.

Did You See What I Saw?
Hoax and Illusion

Two teenagers looking for a little privacy for romance one summer's evening in the early 1990s decided a quiet country lane called Bray Road might be just right. Only a few miles from the little town of Elkhorn, Wisconsin and lined with cornfields and a few farms, it seemed perfectly safe from prying eyes. True, there had been a few rumors around school about some upright, wolf-headed creature stalking the ditches of that area, but the teens reassured each other those were just urban legends.

They pulled their car up next to some bushes just off the road where they wouldn't be easily seen. The hour was late, the farmhouse nearby was dark, and the only sound was the chirping of crickets in the fields. But just as they were about to kiss, the girl jumped back and screamed in horror. Something brown and hairy was hunched right outside the vehicle, trying to peer into the window. As her boyfriend turned his head to see what had frightened her, the creature ran into the bushes. Immediately, the teens decided the legends about the Beast of Bray Road must be true. In moments, they were speeding back toward the safety of the village.

This true story could have been a great witness report, one that helped prove the existence of a werewolf-like creature in Wisconsin, had the creature not been a complete hoax! The hoaxer was renting a

The Furry Popsicle: A Monster Enigma

If unknown, upright furry creatures do exist, where are all the bodies? That question is probably the all-time favorite of modern skeptics, and has always been a thorny riddle for cryptozoologists to ponder. So when a Minnesota man named Frank Hansen turned up with a frozen, unknown, man-like primate body in the late 1960s, researchers were very excited. Here was solid (*frozen* solid!) evidence, it seemed, that the missing link between man and ape really did exist. And if what came to be called the "Minnesota Ice Man" could be proven a new species, then any number of other unexplained furry hominids, manwolves included, might be accepted more easily as flesh and blood realities.

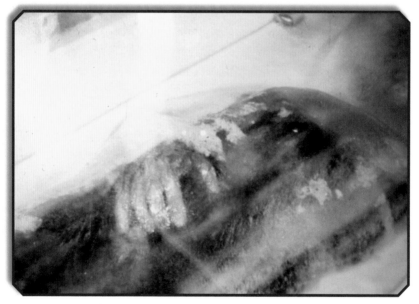

Figure 7.1 *The true nature of the "Minnesota Ice Man" remains a mystery to this day.* (Fortean Picture Library)

"There is a comparatively fresh corpse," wrote researcher and author Ivan T. Sanderson in the May 1969 issue of *Argosy* magazine, "preserved in ice, of a specimen of at least one kind of ultra-primitive, fully-haired man-thing, that displays so many heretofore unexpected and non-human characters as to warrant our dubbing it a 'missing link.'"[61]

Sanderson had been informed that Hansen was exhibiting this creature at fairs and shopping malls around the Midwest, so he went to see it along with Dr. Bernard Heuvelmans, a member of the Belgian Royal Academy of Sciences. Heuvelmans was considered an expert on what was then called the "Abominable Snowman." The men were convinced that the creature, about six feet tall and covered with two- to four-inch brown hair, was genuine and not of any species known to science. They described the nose as "pugged," with wide nostrils. The eyeballs had been "blown out of the sockets," probably by a gun blast (Hansen claimed to have shot it in the 1960 deer hunting season near Aurora, Minnesota). It had very large hands, and its feet were 10 inches wide. "I defy anybody to fool Bernard Heuvelmans on a case like this," argued Sanderson. "You just cannot 'make' a corpse like this, either out of bits and pieces of the bodies of other animals, or of wax, with some half a million hairs inserted into it." Besides, it smelled like rotting flesh.

And yet, the Minnesota Ice Man would eventually be declared a fake by many researchers. The owner kept changing his story as to where and how it had been found, and it was alleged that after Sanderson and Heuvelmans made their examination, the actual body was removed and a poor copy substituted in a new block of ice. Others said the body was faked all along, while a few insisted the change in appearance was due to melting and refreezing of the ice block. Today, neither the original body nor the model of it (if indeed there was a model) is available for examination, and the very heated debate over the Ice Man's authenticity shows no sign of chilling.

farm on Bray Road and had grown sick of teens parking on his property. He had heard the rumors of a manwolf, too, and wanted to put an end to the trespassing. So, he rustled up a gorilla suit, then lay in wait on the next Saturday night for an unwary couple to park on his land. As he crept silently up to the car in his bulky costume, he knew that only a quick glimpse would be necessary to terrorize the young lovers. He was correct, as the frantic teens spread the word of yet another encounter with the Beast.

Of course, there had been many other sightings on Bray Road that could not have been hoaxed, incidents where the witnesses had a clear view of the creature and could see that its head and legs were canine. But knowing that this one case of intentional tomfoolery did happen[62] and that other, similar pranks have been played in other "monster sighting" areas should inspire caution in anyone wishing to research strange creatures.

HYENA GETS THE LAST LAUGH

Whenever something that looks like a werewolf is sighted, local authorities and skeptics supply all sorts of suggestions as to what witnesses might "really" have seen. Sometimes the suggestions are more absurd than the creature they are meant to replace. One animal frequently offered as the possible "true" identity of alleged manwolves is the hyena. The only problem is that a hyena is sorely out of place anywhere in North or South America, where they do not live in the wild. Any hyena spotted there would have to be an escaped zoo, circus, or sanctuary animal.

Animal escapes do sometimes occur. One newspaper in Paulding County, Ohio, reported just such an incident in 1858. The *Cleveland Plain Dealer* declared on February 6 of that year that a circus hyena had broken free in Paulding County and was busily digging up graves and terrorizing those who came in contact with it. The beast had already mauled two men to death, the article said.

After area residents intent on learning the latest about the loose hyena had purchased sufficient newspapers to boost circulation, the reporter confessed that he had made the entire story up.[63] In this particular case, that was the end of it. But it's easy to imagine some intrepid researcher combing old newspapers a century or two later, coming across the hyena headlines but not the reporter's later admission of guilt, and concluding some hyena-like critter had indeed run amok in Paulding County.

This sensationalized case helps prove the adage "Don't believe everything you read"—especially in very old newspapers. Most people don't realize that in the 1800s, most American towns had several highly competitive publications, and it became accepted practice for reporters to write outrageous stories similar to those in today's tabloids to attract readers. It's likely that more than one local legend is the result of uncorrected misinformation like that in the hyena story.

It's good to remember, too, that sometimes animals are simply misidentified. The creature in a widely reported hyena sightings flap around Superior, Wisconsin, in August 2006 turned out to be nothing more than a nearly hairless timber wolf with a bad case of mange.

A bored teenager perpetrated another hoax in 1969 in Calhoun County, Alabama. People driving around rural roads in the area reported seeing a hairy, upright, horned creature dancing in the ditches. It was dubbed the Choccolocco Monster, after Choccolocco Road where it appeared, and it kept locals in a panic for weeks. Finally, the sightings mysteriously stopped. The monster was never explained until 2001, when *Anniston Star* reporter Matthew Creamer announced in a Halloween story that one Neal Williamson had finally come clean about the horned beast. Williamson, 15 at the time of the incidents, had thought he would scare up some fun by donning a long fur coat or a sheet and a cow skull, hiding in the bushes in the dark, then popping out to jig around at passing motorists. He pulled his trick at least four times, but eventually happened to step out in front of someone with a rifle and nearly took a couple of bullets. Luckily, the gunman was a poor shot, but the close shave was enough to convince Williamson to hang up the skull hat forever. [64]

Interestingly, according to Creamer, the creature's description evolved over time as more residents witnessed Williamson's beast. The hair color changed from dark gray to black and white, and the prominent teeth noticed by early witnesses were later said to be hidden by thick, stringy hair. People became more convinced of its reality as sightings continued. Creamer quoted one resident as saying, "I knowed it was the booger." (*Booger* is a folk term for swamp monsters.)

Williamson had some fun with his little monster dance that became the Choccolocco Monster's hallmark. But the good folk of Calhoun County didn't particularly enjoy finding out they had been the collective butt of Williamson's long-guarded, secret joke.

TRUTH OR DARE? WHOM TO BELIEVE?

Stories like the Paulding Hyena and Choccolocco Monster beg the question, how reliable are eyewitness accounts? Can we accept that Bigfoot and werewolf-like creatures exist when all we have may be anecdotal evidence? Skeptics often charge that people are notoriously unreliable when reporting even mundane occurrences or describing other people. And if it can be shown that observers are often mistaken when reporting the appearance of other human beings, can eyewitnesses of unknown creatures be expected to be any more accurate? According to Michael C. Dorf, in an article called "How Reliable is Eyewitness Testimony?", "numerous psychological studies have shown that human beings are not very good at identifying people they saw only once for a relatively short period of time. The studies reveal error rates of as high as 50 percent." Dorf also notes that stress can further diminish the ability of people to identify a stranger. [65]

These studies were conducted on people trying to identify another human in a witness lineup, not a tall, dark, furry thing in the woods. But if the experiment's finding that human powers of observation are not as reliable as we would like to believe they are, then eyewitness stories seem to be rather weak evidence, particularly since few situations are as stressful as encountering a huge, hairy monster! But there are a few important differences to note between the studies of human witness lineups and encounters with strange creatures. In the studies cited by Dorf, no one was trying to figure out whether what they saw was simply human or animal. Instead, participants faced the complex task of trying to match the facial features of a complete stranger to their memory of a quick glimpse of the person.

Eyewitnesses of big furry hominids, on the other hand, are mostly concerned with identifying what kind of creature they sighted. They need not worry about distinguishing one manwolf from another. The difference between the two tasks might lead to different success rates in later recall. Imagine two police lineups. In one, a witness is asked to choose between three Caucasian males around the same height and with brown hair, but with different faces. In the second lineup, the witness is required to point to which creature he or she saw—a bear, a deer, or an upright, wolf-headed thing. It's probable that success rates would be much higher with the second lineup. Something highly unusual is always much easier to remember.

Creature witnesses often say that the image of the creature they saw was burned into their brains, making it unforgettable. And yet, the article quoted above also noted that even witnesses in human trials who insisted they were sure of what they saw were not necessarily more reliable than the more uncertain witnesses. If it can be shown that witness memories are not always completely reliable, then, what physical proof, otherwise known as "hard" evidence, of werewolves exists? Photos or casts of footprints, samples of fur, or feces, or best of all, a specimen of the creature itself, alive or dead, would all fall into this category. With new techniques of DNA analysis, almost any real bit of an animal can yield answers to many questions. So far, though, hard evidence other than footprints has been scant when it comes to Bigfoot, manwolves, sea monsters, and other unknowns.

Those who track these creatures insist they are intelligent enough to obscure their physical traces, perhaps by sticking to hard or leaf-covered ground not soft enough to show footprints. After all, a race of big hairy monsters would need to be very skilled at hiding in order to have stayed out of the human sight for so many centuries. These skills might also include concealing their dead and probably even covering their feces. Still, it's hard to imagine that at least one skeleton or scat pile would not have fallen into human investigative hands at some time.

Finally, even if fur from a manwolf or Bigfoot is some day found, analyzed, and declared to belong to no identifiable creature, its authenticity will remain in question because there is nothing on file to compare it to. No existing laboratory boasts a standard sample of werewolf DNA.

If It Walks Like a Werewolf...

To the average passerby, Eau Claire might look like a perfectly normal, northern Wisconsin town. Lined with homes and businesses within the city limits, the roads turn rural and wooded very quickly as they reach the outskirts. But sometimes, the roads turn spooky, as well.

In the winter of 2004, a man and his son from nearby Mondovi were driving home late from a concert they had attended in Eau Claire when they suddenly found themselves on an unfamiliar, narrow lane surrounded by snowy forests. They traveled about a mile down the road, the 12-year old son growing more nervous by the minute, when their Ford Contour sedan suddenly stopped.

"The engine died but not the radio or the heat," said the father, "so we would wait a minute, crank it, go a little farther, then do that again and again." They finally made it back into town, stopped for a burger, then headed for home once more. Again, they found themselves on the same, treacherous byway. Again the car died, and this time the man hit the brakes and slid, hitting some kind of large, elk-like animal that sniffed at him and then walked into the forest. Terrified, the man and his son tried desperately to get their car going again, with the engine dying every 50 to 100 yards. They had just made it to a sharp turn when the father looked in his rearview mirror and received the shock of his life. "I saw something I've never seen before," he said. "I thought it was a werewolf, and we're not science fiction nerds. He was crossing the road 30 yards behind us on four feet with a weird kind of swagger—his shoulders were doing all the talking. At this point the car is not starting, no energy at all. Then my son turns and notices the thing is now coming toward us. When it saw our car, it did something like the way a horse bucks up, moved its front paws kind of weird, and did a walk on two feet, then came toward us on all fours again."

The man was now frantically trying to turn over the engine, and it finally started when the black-furred creature was about 10 yards away. The man drove around the curve, but the creature followed them on two legs. "It took six or seven steps on two feet," said the father, "and we were both screaming by then. Then it dropped back down to gain speed. At that point, the creature gave up the chase and walked back into the forest.

"It was a mammoth of an animal," he said. "I didn't get a good look at its face but its ears were long with a wild point like a tuft on top. I still don't know what to call it," he added, "but it was *not* a bear, wolf, or dog. I felt it was really after us. It was dumbfounding."

DO THE LOCOMOTION

As this true story taken from the author's files (courtesy of author and researcher Chad Lewis) shows, one characteristic of alleged were-creatures is their ability to walk on either two feet (bipedally) or all fours (quadrupedally). This strikes observers as strange because normally, animals of all types, including man, are designed to walk one way or the other. Humans, for instance, are **bipeds**; human spines and shoulders are not designed to go about on all fours. Human legs are jointed with knees too close to the ground for trotting like a **quadruped**, with heads aligned so that on all fours, they face down instead of ahead. Most other mammals are quadrupeds; even the great apes such as chimpanzees and gorillas normally lean far forward and use their knuckles to propel themselves along the ground. It should be noted that people who have encountered Bigfoot, considered by most to be apelike, always remark that it walks erect and appears to get about very naturally on two feet.

There are a few exceptions to this rule of biped or quadruped. Hopping mammals like the tiny, desert-dwelling gerboa and the kangaroos and wallabies of Australia are bipedal, but not in the easy striding fashion peculiar to humans. Some birds and lizards can actually run on their hind legs, making them technically bipedal, but they would never be mistaken for a wolf man. (That doesn't mean people haven't claimed to have witnessed bird men!)[66]

Also, some quadrupeds do have the ability to stand on their hind legs to eat or survey their surroundings. Bears are known for rearing up momentarily to have a look around them or to reach into a beehive for honey. There is an antelope found in East Africa known as the "Waller's gazelle," or gerenuk, which stands up in order to reach the kind of leaves it enjoys, using its front hooves to hold the branches in place while it feasts. But it doesn't stroll around the jungle on two feet.

PAWS, FOR A MOMENT

Injured or deformed animals can be quite another story, however. On the Web site YouTube.com,[67] one of the most downloaded videos is a *Montel Williams Show* segment on a dog named Faith, born with only stubs for front limbs. Faith was trained by her devoted owner to walk on her hind legs, and was featured on several national television shows. She is shown strolling, not hopping or jumping, down the street next to her owner. Her neck juts forward a bit in keeping with her canine spinal alignment, which makes it interesting to note that manwolf eyewitnesses often assert that although the creature they saw walked naturally, its "neck was hunched over." But the video proves that it is entirely possible for a **canid** to walk on its hind legs if it has sufficient motivation.

Figure 8.1 *Laura Stringfellow, 14, plays with her dog Faith at their home in Oklahoma City. Faith was born with her two front legs badly deformed and learned how to stand up and walk on two legs.* (Stephen Holman/ZUMA/Corbis)

Of course, it's highly unlikely that Faith or any other animal born without forelimbs would be able to survive in the wild. Faith had humans to shelter, feed, and train her. In the wild, she would have had no way to catch food and would have been easy prey for larger carnivores.

It doesn't seem likely, then, that forelimb injury could be a viable explanation for the wild canids that have been seen walking upright. Of all the sightings of upright manwolves, one has yet to be reported as missing front legs or even paws. Indeed, many witnesses have noted the creatures either using their "arms" to carry something such as a piece of animal carcass, or even cupping their paws to sip water.

Perhaps the ability to use its forelimbs to handle food and water would give a wild creature certain advantages. A scavenger or hunter with a meal too big to eat in one sitting would find it easier to carry its food to a safe place using its arms than to drag it by mouth. It would also be more convenient to keep a watch for other predators while dining in an upright position rather than bent close to the ground with a full mouth.

Could it be that a group of canines has been able to adapt their walking posture in order to gain these benefits? If so, it's easy to understand how our occasional glimpses of them going about their

Faith the Bipedal Dog

It was late December 2002 in Oklahoma when a female chow gave birth to a litter of mixed breed puppies, several of them deformed. One, the runt of the litter, was born with one forelimb missing and the other horribly misshapen and useless. Young Reuben Stringfellow, 17 at the time, rescued the pup and took it home to his mother, Jude, who adopted the helpless creature and named her Faith. The deformed leg had to be removed when Faith was seven months old, and the family set about the long task of teaching her to walk on her hind legs. They did this by enticing her to stand for treats.

Faith has since been featured on many national TV shows, from *Inside Edition* to *Oprah*, and the clip from her appearance on the *Montel Williams Show* is one of the most-viewed videos on YouTube.com. Watching Faith walking with her human companions, it is apparent that she is truly striding and not hopping as most deformed animals learn to do.[68] If there ever were an argument that bipedal canids can exist, Faith the Dog™ would have to be considered the best available evidence. Jude Stringfellow wrote a book detailing the plucky pup's story, *With a Little Faith*, and maintains a Web site called FaiththeDog.net.

business in an upright posture could seem so startling and humanlike that they are mistaken for werewolves.

KEEPING BIGFOOT AND MANWOLF ON THEIR TOES

Of course, those who favor the idea that these creatures are supernatural, either changing from human to animal or the other way around, would say that it is only "natural" for the creature to display traits from both sides of the dimensional coin. If a shape-shifter truly has the power to transform bone and muscle into forms other than its own, how hard could it be to go from walking on two feet to running on four?

Thinking a little about the anatomy of legs in actual flesh-and-blood animals, though, also helps to distinguish manwolves from that other big and questionable forest dweller, Bigfoot. Some have speculated that creatures looking like werewolves are actually another form of Bigfoot, just a smaller, Eastern cousin. However, as we noted earlier, Bigfoot descriptions plant the creature firmly in the great ape family. And the footprints of apes have one thing in common: they involve the whole foot, placed flat on the ground. This type of footprint is referred to as **plantigrade**. Bears also make plantigrade footprints.

Wolves, dogs, and cats, however, leave what we call **digitigrade** (using digits, or toes) tracks. Digitigrade trackers walk on their toepads and on what we would call the ball of their foot, with the "heel" joint placed farther up off the ground. Manwolf eyewitnesses, when they have a good look at the legs, will usually note that the "legs were bent backwards." The legs appear that way to them because the creature's heel is high off the ground, placed rather like a human's knee. But a knee bends forward and a heel bends backward, so it looks wrong when the creature walks.

In the few instances where the creatures have left tracks, the difference between dog man and Bigfoot becomes readily apparent. Everyone knows what the huge, flat, humanlike Bigfoot tracks are supposed to look like. Dog man or manwolf tracks look like large-sized dog or wolf prints. It is all the more amazing that bipedal canids are able to get around on those digitigrade hind feet, which are not designed to support their full weight.

In summary, although it is unusual, it is not physically impossible for a canine to walk around on its hind legs. Canine bone structure is consistent with the "hunched" posture and "bent legs" that witnesses report. Perhaps these creatures are a new species after all.

Celebrity Were-mania: Howling with the Stars

In a shadowy corner of a dank, foreboding castle in Transylvania, the raven-haired princess Anna is shocked to suddenly encounter her dead brother, Velkan, looking alive and well, if a bit pale. He gasps that he must tell her something, but before he can finish, the moon rises in an open window, and Velkan begins to convulse. Anna watches, horrified, as her brother throws back his head in agony. His muscles expand and pop, his nose and mouth lengthen into a muzzle with long, pointed fangs, and his clothing bursts off his body to reveal a coat of thick, dark fur. The contortions enable him to run up the stone wall like a fly as he continues to change. Finally, tall, pointed ears rise from the top of his head like thick antennae, and the princess knows what has happened. Her brother was bitten by a werewolf and has become one himself.

Once Velkan's transformation into a slavering manimal is complete, he no longer knows Anna as his sister; she becomes his prey. With astounding agility, the beast springs from floor to ceiling at lightning speed, all the time howling and slashing at her. He has become, to all appearances, an invincible killing machine. It is now up to the legendary stalker of vampires and werewolves, Gabriel Van Helsing, to elude the creature's wicked grasp and hunt down the cruel animal that was once Anna's brother.

This scene from the 2004 Universal Pictures movie *Van Helsing* displays a fantastic assortment of special effects, all designed to portray one of the most powerful versions of the werewolf ever shown in the world of filmmaking. But the classic motifs moviegoers have come to expect in man-beast transformations are all still there: the painful muscle contractions, the expansion of the chest cavity, growth of the muzzle and elongation of the ears, and, most of all, the sprouting of a good, shaggy growth of fur. There are "rules" for werewolves in all media of our popular culture, and for the most part, they are followed to the letter. They also include a grueling conversion scene, wounding with holy water, a gory demonstration of the beast's murderous abilities, and its final end accomplished with a well-aimed silver bullet.

Although werewolves have been part of human lore throughout recorded history, modern culture—specifically, movies like *Van Helsing*—has created the well-muscled powerhouse that is today's Hollywood werewolf. But even film werewolves have undergone an evolution.

The man usually credited with recharging the ancient creature's batteries was Lon Chaney Jr., whose acting skills made the fur-faced, transformed Wolf Man not only fearsome but sympathetic. People were terrified of the werewolf's murdering ways in such early Universal Studios flicks as *The Wolf Man* (1941) but they still *liked* this poorly groomed manwolf. Fitted out with a prosthetic muzzle and a fuzzy thatch of hair that came clear down to his eyebrows, Chaney Jr. in full werewolf makeup was transformed into an American icon, and the lore in his movies became standard werewolf dogma. In fact, Curtis Siodmak, the screenwriter of *The Wolf Man*, wrote this gypsy folk verse into the script...

Even a man who's pure at heart
And says his prayers by night
May become a wolf when the wolfbane blooms
And the autumn moon is bright.

Many accepted the verse as genuine, assuming Siodmak had found it by researching old Romany traditions. Siodmak, however, freely admitted that he made the verse up![69] The 2004 movie, *Van Helsing*, uses the 1941 Siodmak verse word-for-word.

The Wolf Man was not Hollywood's first attempt at a werewolf movie. In 1913, an actual wolf was used for the morphing scene in a silent, black-and-white version titled *The Werewolf*. Only 18 minutes long, the film was based on the Navajo legend of the shape-shifter. And this first of the celluloid werewolves was not only Native American, but a female.

One of the best werewolf movies ever made, many critics will agree, was the 1935 film *Werewolf of London*, released a full six years before Chaney Jr.'s breakthrough role. In this black-and-white Universal picture, London's werewolf was a botanist who happened to be bitten in Tibet while on a quest for the strange Mariphasa plant. Of course, he managed to return to London to run amok. Coincidentally, the flowers of the Mariphasa contained the antidote to werewolfism. As in medieval lore, the tortured botanist/beast returned to human form after being shot by a London policeman.

Since those early ventures, there has been no end of werewolf movies, each striving to stamp its own mark on the genre. There was the werewolf-as-youth twist, for instance, in the 1957 classic *I Was a Teenage Werewolf*, which starred a young Michael Landon. In this movie, Landon's road to werewolfery came from being treated by an evil hypnotherapist. Its "wolfboy" theme was echoed in the comical 1985 flick, *Teen Wolf*, where Michael J. Fox used his werewolf size and strength to dominate his high school basketball team and enhance his popularity.

Other werewolf movies have explored the darker ranges of human-wolf transformation. From *The Howling* (1981), with its cult of backwoods werewolves, to *Dog Soldiers* (2002), about a band of military commandos on a training mission in the Scottish Highlands who find a surprising, wolfen enemy deep in the woods, blood-soaked attacks on humans have become expected fare in modern movie versions. As special effects techniques have advanced, so has the level and sophistication of the portrayal of mangled innards and body parts left in the werewolf's wake.

Moviemakers continue to come up with ingenious additions to the werewolf mythology. Stephen King's *Silver Bullet* (1985) brought religion into the werewolf mix with a man of the cloth as one of the main characters, while she-wolves received new prominence with the *Ginger Snaps* series (2000-2005) about two sisters-in-lycanthropy. And two of the most intensely advertised, *Underworld* (2003) and its sequel, *Underworld: Evolution* (2006) pitted werewolves against vampires as longtime mortal enemies. Were-creatures have also infiltrated films meant for younger viewers, such as Nick Parks's animated film *Curse*

Figure 9.1 An American Werewolf in London *(1981) forever altered Hollywood's depiction of werewolves.* (Photofest)

of the Were-Rabbit (2005), or the film version of *Harry Potter and the Prisoner of Azkaban* (2004), which featured a professor who was really a werewolf.

Werewolves may be around for a while, if movies are to be believed. Mike Martinez's short (23 minutes) 2003 film *Chimera: The Werewolf Cult Chronicles* blasts a saga of fuzzy white manwolves into the year 2019, when mutant beasts roam an icy world suffering from nuclear winter. Having gone that far afield, the legendary creature could literally go anywhere: deepest outer space, the center of the earth, even other dimensions. It's probably safe to say werewolves will visit these places and more before Hollywood has its final way with them.

Television has not been immune to the werewolf's bite. A series called *Wolf Lake* chronicled the bad deeds of a pack of teenage shapeshifters, while *Buffy the Vampire Slayer* had a very sympathetic werewolf character named Oz. To keep from killing his classmates, he kindly locked himself into the school library's back room whenever the moon was full.

Many werewolf movies, such as *The Howling* and *Silver Bullet*, were based on books. There is a whole world of werewolf fiction and non-fiction too vast to cover here, with titles increasing every year as the notion of werewolves becomes ever more popular. Brian J. Frost's *The Essential Guide to Werewolf Literature* is an entire volume devoted to published material on werewolves, including other reference guides, novels, short story anthologies, non-fiction, old "pulp fiction" tales, and more. Frost predicts the werewolf novel will only continue to grow in popularity when he remarks, "There is, after all, nothing more effective than the werewolf story for exploring the murky realm of the unconscious and revealing the awful deeds it can inspire."[70]

PLAYING WOLF

Perhaps Brian J. Frost's insight into the popularity of werewolf novels also reveals why werewolf videos and role-playing games have exploded

Lon Chaney Jr. (1906-1973): The Man Inside the Wolf Man

Legend has it that werewolfism can be passed from one generation to the next. Ironically, Universal Studios's star Wolf Man, Lon Chaney Jr., inherited his talent for *portraying* monsters from his father, Lon Chaney. His dad had become famous for starring in silent horror flicks such as *The Hunchback of Notre Dame* and *The Phantom of the Opera*. But Chaney Jr.'s very entrance into this world was a bit creepy.

Born two months premature on a cold February day in Oklahoma, he appeared to be stillborn. His father Lon ran outside with his tiny, lifeless newborn and dunked the boy into a freezing lake, snapping him to life. His mother was also an actor and called the baby Creighton, after her family name. The young family traveled the country, often using little Creighton as a stage prop in their Vaudeville shows before Lon Chaney made it big in Hollywood. As the elder Chaney aged, he tried to discourage his son from going into the movie business,[71] but Creighton couldn't resist following in his father's oversized footsteps. When Lon Chaney died of a throat hemorrhage in 1930, Creighton rechristened himself as Lon Chaney Jr., and began looking for the same types of roles that had made his father a household name.

The son would eventually surpass his father in monster fame. His film career actually began with just one of his body parts in a 1922 movie called *The Trap*, in which only his hand appeared. After his big leading role in *The Wolf Man* in 1941, he played Frankenstein's monster in *Frankenstein's Ghost*, then the mummy in *The Mummy's Tomb*, *The Mummy's Ghost*, and *The Mummy's Curse*. He also played the Wolf Man character in four more movies. Some of his other, very colorful credits include *Weird Woman*, *Cobra Woman*, *Man-Made Monster*, *Dead Man's Eyes*, *Bride of the Gorilla*, *I Died a Thousand Times*, and *The Alligator People*.

In contrast to his rampaging film roles, Chaney Jr. was said to be easy-going in his private life, fond of fishing and cooking and known as a master storyteller. Chaney Jr. had two sons, but neither seemed to inherit the gene for monstrous charisma. The family acting dynasty ended when Chaney Jr. succumbed to a heart attack in 1973.

But after all the movie-set cemeteries the Wolf Man stalked during his career, no grave was dug for Chaney Jr. at the end of his life. His final wishes for the disposal of his remains seem very appropriate, considering the many lab-created monsters he portrayed. Lon Chaney Jr. willed his body to the University of Southern California for the benefit of science.[72]

Figure 9.2 *Lon Chaney Jr. and Evelyn Akers starred in the classic* The Wolf Man, *which brought the werewolf legend into modern pop culture.* (Underwood & Underwood/Corbis)

in recent years. Naturally, playing the beast is more exciting than reading about it. One of the most successful games is Mark Rein-Hagen's *Werewolf: The Apocalypse*, a complex pastime employing mostly well-intentioned, super-strong, and magical werewolves. Or as Rein-Hagen calls it, "a storytelling game of savage horror."[73] Part graphic novel and part rule and character guide, it sets up a race called "Garou," with traits such as ability to shape-shift, immunity to wounds, heightened senses of smell and hearing, and frenzied emotions.

"*Werewolf* combines a Gothic ambience of horror with a *film noir*, punk world of pollution and decay," explains Rein-Hagen. And he's right; the world of the *Garou* draws on both European medieval lore and many of the modern werewolf conventions examined above.

Video, of course, can ratchet up the levels of fantasy and violence considerably. *Altered Beast*, one of the earliest werewolf video games, took arcades by storm when it debuted in 1988, and also enjoyed some popularity in home video games. In this game, the heroic human enjoyed turning into a werewolf with many powers once a certain level of victory over various demons and other nasties was achieved, but no biting was necessary for transformation. The powers were conferred or taken away courtesy of a manipulative sorcerer.

A more recent video game, Gabriel Knight's *The Beast Within* for Sierra, takes realism in games a step farther with live actors shown on site in Germany, blending the modern look with much traditional lore and mythology. And in many games, the werewolf is just one of many characters, often with an interesting history. *Baldur's Gate II* includes a shape-shifting druid named Cernd who is able to wreak vengeance on enemies by tracking them in the form of a wolf.

These are just a few examples of the many games available with werewolves as important characters. It is easy to find them and others, along with fan sites, discussion boards, and more on the Internet, a fluid medium which suits shape-shifting beings perfectly. As much as books or movies have done, werewolf games help keep the ancient lore of the druid and berserker alive in modern times.

THE COMIC BOOK WOLFMAN

Finally, one other influential source of werewolf art and legend must be noted. It would be hard to imagine the well-muscled, glowering werewolves that inhabit role-playing manuals and leap through the digital castles of video games without a firm foundation of comic art first having given them shape. Comic artists have drawn on the Hollywood fantasy of the towering, hairy he-man to design a creature that snarls off the page at readers.

Werewolves were popular comic book creatures during the 1940s and early 1950s. The EC line of comic books, including *The Haunt of Fear*, *Tales from the Crypt*, and *The Vault of Horror*, often featured werewolves, along with many other classic monsters like vampires and zombies. When the 1954 Comics Code set new guidelines for comic book content, though, werewolves and many other horrific elements were banned.

In the early 1970s, comics magazine publishers who were not subject to the Code due to their large-size format, reintroduced werewolves and other monsters in their stories, weakening the authority of the Code and paving the way for the return of werewolves in full. Marvel Comics was the alpha leader of this pack.

One of their best-known lycanthropes was Man-Wolf, a character in Marvel's *Spider-man* series. Man-Wolf first showed up in *The Amazing Spider-man* #124 when a Moon rock turned the son of J. Jonah Jameson into a werewolf. Another Marvel comics star, Captain America, briefly transformed into a creature named Capwolf for one storyline. Marvel also issued the series *Werewolf By Night*, which chronicled the adventures of Jack Russell, a young California man who turned into a werewolf each month due to an ancestral curse. Considered by many readers to be the definitive werewolf comic book, *Werewolf By Night* remains popular today.

There are too many other classic werewolf comics to list here, but a few others of interest include Eternity's *Werewolf at Large*, where the Lycan's sidekick is his psychic granny, and Antarctic Press's *Gold Digger*, which features a were-cheetah and a clutch of werewolves. Many Japanese *manga* series take on assorted were-beasts. The idea of shape-shifting is a common theme in comic books, where it is depicted in a variety of forms, many of which owe their inspiration at least indirectly to werewolf legend and lore.

10

Your Field Guide to Werewolves

The night was as black as a timber wolf's nose, and we huddled together near the woods with flashlights at the ready as the howling and yipping noises came closer. It sounded like at least half a dozen animals were approaching us in the darkness. We had not brought guns, pepper spray, or any other weapons, and couldn't help but wonder if it was really so smart to be spending a night in a desolate farm field where an upright, wolf-headed creature had been spotted barely a month before.

We stood, that night, between a freshly planted cornfield and the Wisconsin state wildlife refuge area known as the Lima Marsh. Only a few weeks earlier, a college senior on her way home late at night from her job as a movie theater clerk was shocked to see what looked like a bipedal wolf running across Highway 59 in eastern Rock County, Wisconsin. It was headed straight for the field where we now waited.

The woman had gone straight to her computer and Googled terms related to "werewolf" until she found contact information for the *Beast of Bray Road* site, and then wrote to ask what she might have seen. This was an exciting e-mail to receive, because the great majority of sighting reports are made months or even years later, after the trail has long grown cold. And often, they are in distant places or on inaccessible land. By a stroke of very good fortune, this one happened to be near the farm of some people I knew, and who kindly gave me permission to bring a team of investigators for an overnight stakeout.

The seven of us baited the area with chicken pieces and open cans of cat food. We placed motion-activated cameras in key spots, and used walkie-talkies to communicate as we fanned out in pairs to cover the area. We hadn't seen anything unusual all night, though, until we decided to sit quietly together, lights off, in one final attempt to catch a glimpse of the unknown creature. And now, a howling pack of canids was coming our way.

Coyotes, we finally decided. Sounding less than friendly. Perhaps it was best not to let them sneak up on us after all. We turned our floodlights on, aimed them at where the sound had come from…and saw nothing but a dark hillside! Supreme escape artists that they are, the coyotes had vanished. Perhaps the manwolf fled with them. At any rate, he had eluded us that night. Still, I was glad to have made the effort when such a golden opportunity presented itself, and everyone involved was satisfied we had given it our best shot.

TO HUNT OR NOT TO HUNT?

The question does need to be asked: is it really such a great idea to trek out into the wilderness or some lonely farm field in hopes of getting that first film or photo of a manwolf or any other monstrous creature, for that matter? If the answer lies in whether the odds of success are likely to be high or not, then there are probably far smarter ways to spend a spring evening. It is very seldom that creature-seekers are rewarded with so much as a stray hair or anomalous footprint, much less a clear photo or video. The vast majority of sightings are seemingly random, chance occurrences and almost never happen when planned.

A strong argument could be made that an equally valid form of creature-hunting can be done via the Internet, books, and other

Figure 10.1 *Kevin Nelson and Noah Voss use binoculars for a better look at their quarry while communicating with other search party members via walkie-talkies.* (Author's Collection)

media, without ever setting foot into beast-haunted woods. This method is likely to yield far more information, and is a much safer and cheaper means of investigation than traveling to strange sites with lots of equipment. Probably for the vast majority of people, it's the only truly workable way to research monsters and is very rewarding in its own right.

Adventurous people with strong curiosity about the many reported sightings of unknown beasts will still probably try to see one for themselves at some point. Bearing in mind that it's likely the only wild creatures encountered will be possums or raccoons, there are many important things to consider before setting off on a creature safari. The first question probably concerns where to look.

FINDING THE HABITRAIL

To begin, permission is required before anyone sets foot on private land. And even some public parks and wildlife areas have posted time restrictions, or demand that state park stickers be purchased before using the area.

The prospective creature hunter should also study likely habitats of the intended target. In the case of the manwolf, it is almost always seen fairly close to some body of water. It appears to follow rivers, and is often spotted near marshes. It normally remains near dense cover, such as a thickly wooded area. Cornfields are another preferred hangout, since they make excellent hiding places and are full of deer and other game filling up on ripe corn. Cornfields are always on private land, however, and it is very easy to get lost in one.

It may be helpful to search out spots where the creature has been seen previously, in hopes that it will keep returning. But keep in mind that any large carnivore will have the capability to roam widely, and that hotspots of anomalous creature sightings tend to move over time. What may have once been the likeliest place to look for a creature is likely to have lost its edge a decade later.

FAUNA FAMILIARITY

One of the best ways to prepare to identify unknown animals is to bone up on all the *known* animals that might be encountered at any given spot. Knowing what is supposed to be in that cornfield or woods, from field mice to white-tailed deer, makes it much easier to identify anything that is truly out of the ordinary.

Besides memorizing the physical descriptions of local wildlife, the well-prepped hunter will also be ready to recognize their spoor by knowing the "Three Fs": footprints, feces, and fur. It's also good to understand which animals might be potentially dangerous, and how best to deal with them. The safest bet is to consult your own state wildlife experts or game wardens for animal information specific to your locale.

At the location we explored in the example above, the crew had done its homework and was pretty sure the largest carnivore in the area would be the coyote. But it is always possible that feral dogs could be prowling in any part of the country, as well. And while bigger animals like bears, timber wolves, and mountain lions are still rare in places like southern Wisconsin, they are becoming more frequent visitors there and in many other places where they haven't been seen in years. As humans encroach on their turf, they are forced to invade our populated areas. Unfortunately, there is still a bigger chance you will run into one of these natural creatures than a Sasquatch or manwolf.

GEARING UP

So let's say you've identified a prime creature-hunting spot, cleared your legal passage through the area, and are ready to see a bona fide beast. Unlike our cave-dwelling ancestors, who had to take their chances on meeting mastodon or giant puma with only handmade weapons and their usual change of clothing, we have a wide array of field gear available to us, from protective clothing to electronic monitoring devices.

Smart hunters will take advantage of as much helpful equipment as possible, starting with the basic element of body coverings.

Dressing appropriately for the weather and terrain might seem like a very obvious point, but I've learned that not everyone "gets" this concept. While all of the experienced crew on our Lima Marsh Monster stakeout were wisely clad in hiking boots and rain-repellent jackets on that cool, misty spring evening, I've had people on other excursions show up in a northern, forested area wearing shorts and flip-flops. The mosquitoes ate them alive before any monster had a chance at them.

Besides mosquitoes, there are always ticks, deer flies, spiders, snakes, and other mini-beasts from which you will want protection. A hat is always a good idea, and long pants and sleeves are usually preferable to short ones unless you're in a superheated desert. And don't forget the bug spray. Look for one that is formulated for "deep woods" and that specifies protection from ticks. Tuck your pant legs into your boots if possible so that creepy-crawlies can't get up inside your jeans.

Noah Voss and Kevin Nelson, Wisconsin investigators who specialize in techno-search teams, also advise leaving your trek wardrobe hanging outdoors for a few days so that it has a more natural scent, and that you refrain from wearing perfumed products or deodorants. That way, you are more likely to remain undetected even if downwind from a sharp-nosed creature.

The end result of all this may not be your idea of a cool fashion statement, but you just might save yourself from getting Lyme disease, severe scratches from twigs, and a whole rash of itchy bug bites. A person can stay in the woods much longer when physical discomfort is not a big issue, and the more time spent there, the greater the likelihood of seeing something unusual.

TOOLS OF THE TRADE

Once dressed for hunting **cryptids**, you'll need a bag or backpack (backpacks leave your hands free for scribbling notes, using equipment, or making frantic sign language to a creature as it is carrying you off) to stow all your personal gear. If you are camping or planning to be in an isolated area for more than a few hours, you will doubtless want more personal items and a supply of food and water, but we will cover only the necessary gear for finding and discovering creature evidence here. For starters

- a 6-12 inch, non-transparent ruler or tape measure to measure evidence and to use in photos as a gauge for size
- one or two flashlights and extra batteries
- a multi-purpose knife such as a Leatherman™
- binoculars
- a notepad and several pens or pencils for recording data
- tweezers for removing evidence such as fur samples
- zip-closing plastic bags from small to very large to contain samples
- a compass and, if available, a GPS unit for recording locations of evidence and, hopefully, creatures
- a working camera and/or camcorder with extra batteries and film or storage media (you may want some cardboard disposable cameras as backups)
- a tape recorder, preferably with external mike, and extra batteries
- clear plastic sheeting (a shower curtain liner works great) in case there are footprints or other things you wish to protect from the elements
- latex gloves for gathering DNA specimens
- a small camper-style shovel in case you need to dig or scoop something
- a sturdy walking stick, preferably with a pointed tip, for hiking aid and possible self-defense (check with local game wardens for other suggestions in this category)

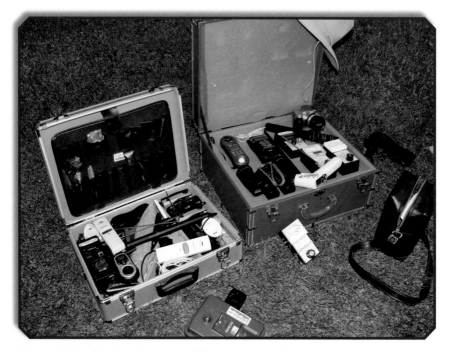

Figure 10.2 *Modern-day werewolf hunters use high-tech gear to find their elusive target.* (Author's Collection)

In addition, you will want to have some other things with you in your vehicle. An important item is plaster of Paris, a jug of water, a large stick or spoon, and a bucket to mix them in so you can make casts of footprints. Practice mixing this in the right proportions and letting it set ahead of time, or you could end up ruining the best manwolf footprint ever found with plaster soup that takes eons to harden, and then breaks into pieces.

You may also want to bring motion-activated "game" cameras, if available. Noah Voss, who owns a Web site devoted to creature-hunting equipment called GetGhostGear.com, advises situating each one with careful thought toward the target animal's height. "There will be an ideal height, angle, and picture-capturing range that is specific for each camera," says Voss.

Getting an image of something is much more likely when bait is placed nearby. Some pieces of "ripe" chicken, open cans of cat food, or any type of meat that's been allowed to get a little smelly will do. Again, place it so that an animal will have to put itself within camera range if it wants the treat.

SPOOKY SUPPLIES

But what if, as we have discussed in some earlier chapters, these creatures really are some type of "paranormal" being—spirit creatures, as some Native American traditions claim, or true shape-shifters conjured through magic, or even visitors from another dimension? If so, they aren't likely to do you any physical harm, which is the good news. The bad news is they are not so likely to show up on your cameras. Still, try to take pictures of any unusual phenomena just in case. And if you are seriously interested in hunting for this type of entity, then you may want to invest in a trifield meter, which can measure three types of invisible waves: magnetic, electric, and radio/microwave. Most paranormal investigators agree that supernatural phenomena are associated with enhanced electromagnetic (EM) force; so high EM readings might indicate an area you will want to check out or perhaps steer clear of!

In addition, John Michael Greer in his book, *Monsters*, advises bringing some sort of sharp iron object, such as a long nail or a silver tip on your walking stick, to jab at any supernatural beings. He notes, "A knife, a nail, a sword, or any other sharp iron object, thrust into a concentration of etheric energy, will cause something not unlike an etheric short-circuit, dispersing the ether and obliterating whatever patterns may have been present in it."[74] Greer also recommends carrying a bottle of holy water, "banishing incense," and other aids to the magic rituals described in his book. All of these recommendations, of course, are strictly subject to your own personal belief system, and are not guaranteed to bring any results.

No one can guarantee, either, that a given person will have the opportunity to witness a werewolf or any other strange creature. And even if such an event does occur, prepare for the likelihood that short of dragging a live specimen back into town with you, it's probable that no evidence you produce will convince the world that these creatures truly exist. Also, keep in mind that some witnesses wish, for one reason or another, that their encounter had never happened. Confronting the unknown can be a very unsettling experience.

But for those who believe that something upright and furry does stalk the woods and cornfields of the civilized and uncivilized world, there may be no alternative but to keep eyes peeled and cameras ready. At this writing, the first confirmed photo of a real-life werewolf is still waiting to be taken.

Timeline

80,000–8,000 BCE   Dire wolves existed in North America

75,000   First known evidence of early human religious activities indicating cult of bear worship

10,000   Wild dogs are domesticated

6500   The civilization of Catal Huyuk in present-day Asia Minor created wall paintings of vulture-priests and of creatures with both human and animal parts

3000   Ancient Egyptians known to worship Anubis, the jackal-headed god of the dead

2000   The Sumerian Epic of Gilgamesh is written, including character Enkidu, a hairy "wild man"

800 BCE–1200 CE   Animal effigy mounds are constructed in Wisconsin and nearby states in the shapes of many creatures important to tribal lore

c. 50   Roman writer Petronius writes early werewolf story, *The Banquet of Trimalchio*

c. 430   St. Patrick is reputed to change a clan of Irishmen into werewolves

1200   Swedish historian Snorri Sturluson writes of berserkers, warriors who wore bear and wolf skins into battle and fought like enraged animals

1484   Pope Innocent VIII issues a proclamation giving power to hunt and kill witches

1486   The *Malleus Maleficarum*, or "Witch Hammer," is published, not only including the pope's decree but spelling out offenses and punishments for accused witches, shape-shifters, and sorcerers

c. 1500–1700   The approximate duration of the European witch trials

mid–1500s   Greek werewolf cults worshipping Zeus and Apollo still exist

1542   A severe outbreak of lycanthropic citizens in Constantinople forces Solyman II to execute at least 150 of the ravening "beasts" around that city

1589   The famous German "werewolf" Peter Stumpf (also Stubb or Stubbe) is tried and executed by torturous methods

1603   Jean Grenier is tried for werewolfism in France, sentenced to life in a friary rather than execution

1700s–early 1800s   Legends of *loup-garou* are told by French emigrants in Detroit, Michigan and Green Bay, Wisconsin

1764   The Beast of Gevaudan, a vicious, large, wolf-like creature, terrorizes part of France, killing many animals and humans until it is killed itself and paraded through a town

1790   A werewolf-like creature kills horse, livestock, and two transient people in North Wales

1838–c. 1880   Cheyenne Dog Soldiers (Hotamitaneo), elite tribal warriors, ride the western plains of the United States and are said to have the ability to shift into wolfen form

1850s   A bipedal wolf attacked a woman in Clinton County, Pennsylvania—a story later told by her nephew Peter Penz

1858   An escaped hyena hoax perpetrated by newspaper in Paulding County, Ohio, terrifies people living in the area, after the animal is falsely reported to be digging up graves and attacking people

1880s   Dog man legends begin in Michigan lumber camp stories

1913   Black-and-white movie *The Werewolf* is made using a live wolf

1918   British officer in Nigeria observed were-hyena predation

1920   Amala and Kamala, wolf girls, are discovered in termite mound in India and announced to the world as true feral children

1936   The earliest reported sighting of a werewolf-like creature in Wisconsin, as an upright canid is seen digging in an Indian

Mound on two occasions behind St. Coletta Institute, Jefferson County, by a night watchman. The creature stands upright and utters a Word-like sound, "Gadara."

1938   A doglike creature on two feet confronts Robert Fortney on the banks of the Muskegon River near Paris, Mecosta County, Michigan

1951   An ergot-poisoning epidemic in Pont-Saint-Esprit, France, leads to a mass outbreak of "werewolf fever"

1960s   Minnesotan Frank Hansen exhibits a frozen, manlike mystery primate known as the Minnesota Ice Man at fairs, carnivals, and shopping malls around the midwestern United States

1960s   A hunter is chased by fanged *santu sakai* in Malaysia

1969   A teenager with a cow skull and fur coat hoaxes several monster appearances on Choccolocco Road in Calhoun County, Alabama

1972   Six Edgerton, Wisconsin teens see an upright wolf creature materialize near a lake cottage

1987   Dog Man is blamed for attack on a cabin near Luther, Michigan, when scratches are found seven feet off the ground but the only footprints look like those of a huge dog

1989   Lori Endrizzi sees a creature kneeling by the side of Bray Road, Elkhorn, Wisconsin, holding "roadkill" in its upturned paws

Early 1990s   A farmer hoaxes a "monster" appearance on Bray Road

October 31, 1991   Doris Gipson, sees an upright, wolf-headed creature near cornfield on Bray Road, running upright, lunging for her car

April 1994   A strange creature changing from wolf to bear is witnessed by two young girls on their parents' farm outside of Maribel in northeastern Wisconsin

December 2002   Faith the Bipedal Dog is born without forelimbs in Oklahoma and learns to walk upright after many training sessions with her owners

May 2003 A young man in Eau Claire, Wisconsin, reports seeing a phantom manwolf in his apartment

Summer 2003 Katie Zahn and three friends are chased by a manwolf and see three other similar but smaller creatures drinking from a stream near Avon Bottoms, Wisconsin

June 2004 Two New York State brothers observe a pair of manwolves running alongside the highway near Plattsburgh, New York

Winter 2004 Mondovi, Wisconsin, man and son are chased in their car by a wolf creature running alternately on two and four legs

June–July 2005 A Georgia funeral director encounters manwolf in a swamp on two separate occasions and records (in a drawing) the huge, doglike footprints he finds nearby

April 2006 Three witnesses observe two different dog men in a forested area near Reed City, Michigan

July 2006 A young man sees a bipedal wolf standing in a ditch in St. Joseph County, Michigan, and then watches it crawl on its stomach into a cornfield

Glossary

ANECDOTAL EVIDENCE   Evidence based on personal accounts of events rather than physical proof

BERSERKERS   Viking warriors who wore the skins of animals into battle; sometimes believed to have the ability to take the actual shape of those animals

BIGFOOT   Term for a large, scientifically unknown apelike creature that walks erect and bipedally and is famous for leaving giant (often 18 inches long or greater), flat footprints that otherwise resemble human tracks; other names include Sasquatch and Yeti

BIPED   An animal that habitually walks on its two hind limbs (bipedally)

BOUDAS   The were-hyena of the Moroccan Berbers

CANID   Any member of the family *Canidae*, including dogs, wolves, or foxes

CHICHWEYA   The were-hyena of southern Africa, which were believed to grow snouts out of the tops of their heads

CONGENITAL HYPERTRICHOSIS   A rare, inherited condition in which long hair covers over 90 percent of the body and face

CRYPTID   A mysterious or hidden creature

CRYPTOZOOLOGISTS   Researchers who study hidden or mysterious animals

DIGITIGRADE   A term referring to animals whose feet contact the ground only with their toes and toe pads, such as dogs, wolves, and cats

DOG MAN   Term for a creature that has the general appearance of a large dog but walks upright like a human

ERGOT A cereal fungus that may cause hallucinations and erratic behavior in humans

ETHERIC ENERGY An unknown type of energy field that some believe comprises the "bodies" of spirit or phantom creatures

EXCARNATION A funerary tradition of stripping corpses clean of flesh by exposing them to the elements and animal predation

FERAL CHILDREN Children found living without human parents and lacking knowledge of human society; often supposed to have been raised by wild animals such as wolves

KITSUNE A Japanese fox demon that often assumes the form of a beautiful woman

LOUP-GAROU A French term for werewolf, or, in parts of the southern United States, may also denote a curse intended to turn its victim into a wild animal

LYCANTHROPE (SHORT FORM, LYCAN) A person who believes he or she may turn spiritually and/or bodily into a wolf, from the Greek King Lycaon, who was changed into a werewolf by the gods

LYCANTHROPY A mental disorder and form of schizophrenia that causes delusions of bodily transformation into a wolf, accompanied by aggressive changes in posture, gesture, and sometimes in eating habits, with a preference shown for raw meat

MAGICIANS People who use incantations, rituals, and other means to achieve results that appear supernatural in origin

MANWOLF A creature that has a body and head of a wolf, but is able to walk and run bipedally like a human

MEGAFAUNA Prehistoric, giant animals including larger-sized versions of many species still existing

METEMPSYCHOSIS The idea that the spirits of men and animals can migrate from one host to another

PLANTIGRADE Refers to animals that walk using the entire sole of the foot, such as men or bears

PORPHYRIA A genetic disorder that can cause a variety of symptoms including psychosis, epileptic seizures, and extreme sensitivity to light

QUADRUPED   An animal that habitually walks on all four limbs (quadrupedally)

SANTU SAKAI   Monstrous, fanged mystery creatures of Kuala Lumpur in Malaysia

SHAMAN   A priest, medicine man, or other supernatural practitioner employing methods such as trance, ritual, hallucinogenic substances, dance, or incantations, often to obtain knowledge of the spiritual realm or effect changes in the physical world

SHAPE-SHIFTER   A person or creature that can change from one form to another, especially by supernatural means

SUMANGAT   The word for the human soul sometimes believed stolen by were-dogs on the island of Timor

TELEPATHY   The transference of thoughts or ideas directly from one mind to another by unknown means

THERIANTHROPY   The belief that a human can transform into an animal, often applied to those who believe they transform spiritually rather than physically

VARGR   A berserker who turned into a werewolf

VOUKOUDLAKS   Eastern European werewolves that lived in tombs like vampires

WAARWOLF   A German dialect word for werewolf

YENALDLOOSHI   Navajo term for a shape-shifting type of magician, usually with evil connotations

Endnotes

1. Elliott O'Donnell, *Werewolves* (Whitefish, Mont.: Kessinger Publishing, 2003).

2. *Mystical Worldwide Web*, "Wolf," *The Mystic's Menagerie*. Available online. URL: http://www.mystical-www .co.uk/animal/animalw.htm#WOL. Downloaded on January 17, 2007.

3. Linda Lyons, "Paranormal Beliefs Come (Super)Naturally to Some," *Gallup Poll*. Available online. URL: http://poll.gallup.com/content/ default.aspx?ci=19558&VERSION=p. Posted on November 1, 2005.

4. Linda S. Godfrey, *Hunting the American Werewolf* (Madison, Wisc.: Prairie Oak Press [Trails Books], 2006), 167-170.

5. Clarissa Pinkola Estes, *Women Who Run with the Wolves* (New York: Ballantine Books, 1996), 27-34.

6. Fred Alan Wolf, *The Eagle's Quest: A Physicist's Search for Truth in the Heart of the Shamanic World* (New York: Summit Books, 1991).

7. Kathryn A. Edwards, ed., *Werewolves, Witches and Wandering Spirits: Traditional Beliefs and Folklore in Early Modern Europe* (Kirksville, Miss.: Truman State University Press, 2002), xv.

8. Linda S. Godfrey, *Hunting the American Werewolf* (Madison, Wisc.: Prairie Oak Press [Trails Books], 2006), 125-131.

9. Ian Woodward, *The Werewolf Delusion* (New York: Paddington Press, 1979), 239.

10. Linda S. Godfrey, *Hunting the American Werewolf* (Madison, Wisc.: Prairie Oak Press [Trails Books], 2006), xiii.

11. Robert Hunter and Jerry Garcia, "The Dire Wolf," *Working Man's Dead* (Claremont, Calif.: Rhino Records).

12. *Wolf History.* "Canis dirus – Dire Wolf," Available online. URL: http://www.naturalworlds.org/ wolf/history/Canis_dirus.htm. Downloaded on January 17, 2007.

13. Linda S. Godfrey, *The Beast of Bray Road: Tailing Wisconsin's Werewolf* (Black Earth, Wisc.: Prairie Oak Press [Trails Books], 2003), 172-173;
Sam D. Gill, and Irene E. Sullivan, *Dictionary of Native American Mythology* (New York: Oxford University Press, 1992), 358.

14. Linda S. Godfrey, *Hunting the American Werewolf* (Madison, Wisc.: Trails Books, Prairie Oak Press, 2006, 105.

15. Linda S. Godfrey, *The Beast of Bray Road: Tailing Wisconsin's Werewolf*

(Black Earth, Wisc.: Prairie Oak Press [Trails Books], 2003), 167-170.

16. Henry R. Schoolcraft, *The Hiawatha Legends, North American Indian Lore* (Gwinn, Mich.: Avery Color Studios, 2001), 116-119.

17. John Bierhorst, *The Mythology of North America* (New York: Oxford University Press. 2002), 214-220.

18. Brad Steiger, *The Werewolf Book: The Encyclopedia of Shape-Shifting Beings* (Farmington Hills, Mich.: Visible Ink Press, 1999), 147.

19. Jamie Hall, *Half Human, Half Animal: Tales of Werewolves and Related Creatures* (Bloomington, Ind.: Authorhouse [privately published], 2003), 186-188.

20. Ibid., 189-190.

21. Patricia Dale-Green, *Lore of the Dog* (Boston, Mass.: Houghton Mifflin, 1967), 143.

22. Brad Steiger, *The Werewolf Book: The Encyclopedia of Shape-Shifting Beings* (Farmington Hills, Mich.: Visible Ink Press, 1999), 235-236.

23. Rosemary Ellen Guiley, *The Encyclopedia of Vampires, Werewolves, and Other Monsters* (New York: Checkmark Books 2005), 172.

24. Jan Knappert, *Pacific Mythology: An Encyclopedia of Myth and Legend* (London, England: Diamond Books, 1995), 322.

25. Montague Summers, *The Werewolf in Lore and Legend* (Mineola, N.Y.: Dover Publications, 2003), 232-234.

26. Adam Douglas, *The Beast Within: A History of the Werewolf* (New York: Avon Books, 1992), 183.

27. Ibid., 46.

28. Ibid., 44.

29. Ibid., 94.

30. Peter Andreas Munch, translated from Norwegian by Sigurd Bernhard Hustvedt, *Norse Mythology: Legends of Gods and Heroes* (New York: The American Scandinavian Foundation, 1963), 107.

31. Kathryn A. Edwards, ed., *Werewolves, Witches and Wandering Spirits: Traditional Beliefs and Folklore in Early Modern Europe* (Kirksville, Miss.: Truman State University Press, 2002), xv.

32. Montague Summers, *The Werewolf in Lore and Legend* (Mineola, N.Y.: Dover Publications, 2003), 205.

33. H.R. Trevor-Roper, *The European Witch Craze of the 16th and 17th Centuries and Other Essays* (New York: Harper and Row, 1967), 92.

34. Kathryn A. Edwards, ed., *Werewolves, Witches and Wandering Spirits: Traditional Beliefs and Folklore in Early Modern Europe* (Kirksville, Miss.: Truman State University Press, 2002), 4.

35. Ibid., 248.

36. Ibid., 148.

37. Ian Woodward, *The Werewolf Delusion* (New York: Paddington Press, 1979).

38. Montague Summers, *The Werewolf in Lore and Legend* (Mineola, N.Y.: Dover Publications, 2003), 223.

39. Linda S. Godfrey, *The Beast of Bray Road: Tailing Wisconsin's Werewolf* (Black Earth, Wisc.: Prairie Oak Press [Trails Books], 2003), 8-9.

40. Linda S. Godfrey, *"Sightings Logs," The Beast of Bray Road Official Site.* Available online. URL: http://www .beastofbrayroad.com/sightingslog. html. Updated December 2006.

41. Deborah Morse-Kahn, *A Guide to the Archaeology Parks of the Upper Midwest* (Lanham, Md.: Roberts Rinehart, 2003), 5.

42. Robert A. Birmingham and Leslie Eisenberg, *Indian Mounds of Wisconsin* (Madison, Wisc.: University of Wisconsin Press, 2000), 67.

43. Linda S. Godfrey, *Hunting the American Werewolf* (Madison, Wisc.: Prairie Oak Press [Trails Books], 2006), xii.

44. Lois Beuler, *Wild Dogs of the World* (New York: Stein and Day, 1973), 62.

45. Adam Douglas, *The Beast Within: A History of the Werewolf* (New York: Avon Books, 1992), 251.

46. Rosemary Ellen Guiley, *The Encyclopedia of Vampires, Werewolves and Other Monsters* (New York: Checkmark Books, 2005), 191.

47. Ibid., 192.

48. Ellen McCrady, *The Ergot Epidemic* in *Mold Reporter,* from *Mold in Human History,* originally published as part of "Mold: The Whole Picture, Pt. 1," *Abbey Newsletter* 23 #4. Available online. URL: http:// www.moldreporter.org/vol1no6/ moldHist. Posted in 1999.

49. Ian Woodward, *The Werewolf Delusion* (New York: Paddington Press, 1979), 124.

50. Linda S. Godfrey, *Hunting the American Werewolf* (Madison, Wisc.: Prairie Oak Press [Trails Books], 2006), 21-22.

51. David Walks-as-Bear, "Bear's Den," *The White Lake Beacon* (Whitehall, MI: November 6, 2005).

52. John Fiske, "Werewolves and Swan-Maidens," *The Atlantic Monthly* 28 (August 1871): 131.

53. Linda S. Godfrey, *Hunting the American Werewolf* (Madison, Wisc.: Prairie Oak Press [Trails Books], 2006), 134-138.

54. Patricia Dale-Green, *Lore of the Dog.* (Boston, Mass.: Houghton Mifflin, 1967), 89.

55. Kathryn A. Edwards, ed., *Werewolves, Witches and Wandering Spirits: Traditional Beliefs and Folklore in Early Modern Europe* (Kirksville, Miss.: Truman State University Press, 2002), 36-37.

56. Linda S. Godfrey, *Hunting the American Werewolf* (Madison, Wisc.: Prairie Oak Press [Trails Books], 2006), 120-121.

57. Ibid., 13-18.

58. John A. Keel, *The Complete Guide to Mysterious Beings* (New York: Tor Books, 2002), 8.

59. Robb Riggs, *In the Big Thicket: On the Trail of the Wild Man* (New York: Paraview Press, 2001), 98.

60. Paul Deveraux, *Haunted Land: Investigations into Ancient Mysteries and Modern Day Phenomena* (London, England: Piatkus, 2001), 18.

61. Ivan Sanderson, "The Missing Link," *Argosy* (May 1969): 23-31.

62. Linda S. Godfrey, *Hunting the American Werewolf* (Madison, Wisc.: Prairie Oak Press [Trails Books], 2006), 267-268.

63. Alex Boese, *Museum of Hoaxes: A Collection of Pranks, Stunts, Deceptions and Other Wonderful Stories Contrived for the Public from the Middle Ages to the New Millennium.* (New York, N.Y.: Dutton, 2002), 74

64. Linda S. Godfrey, *The Beast of Bray Road: Tailing Wisconsin's Werewolf* (Black Earth, Wis.: Prairie Oak Press [Trails Books], 2003), 159.

65. Michael C. Dorf, *How Reliable is Witness Testimony?* Findlaw for Legal Professionals. Available online. URL: http://writ.news.findlaw.com/dorf/20010516.html. Posted on May 16, 2001.

66. Linda S. Godfrey, *Hunting the American Werewolf* (Madison, Wisc.: Prairie Oak Press [Trails Books], 2006), 245-247.

67. "Faith – Walking Dog," *You Tube.* Available online. URL: http://www.youtube.com/watch?v=7d_vRGuHVzQ. Posted on April 3, 2006.

68. Jude Stringfellow, *Faith the Biped Dog.* Available online. URL: http:// www.faiththedog.net. Updated on Jan. 14, 2007.

69. Adam Douglas, *The Beast Within; A History of the Werewolf.* New York: Avon Books, 1992, 300.

70. Brian J. Frost, *The Essential Guide to Werewolf Literature* (Madison, Wisc.: University of Wisconsin Press, 2003), xii.

71. Adam Douglas, *The Beast Within: A History of the Werewolf* (New York: Avon Books, 1992), 294.

72. Chaney Entertainment, Inc. "Lon Chaney, Jr. Biography," *The Official Web Site of Lon Chaney and Lon Chaney, Jr.* Available online. URL: http://www.lonchaney.com. Downloaded on Jan. 18, 2007.

73. Mark Rein-Hagen, *Werewolf: The Apocalypse, Second Edition* (Stone Mountain, Calif.: White Wolf Game Studio, 1994), 3.

74. John Michael Greer, *Monsters: An Investigator's Guide to Magical Beings* (St. Paul, Minn.: Llewellyn, 2002), 222.

Further Resources

WEB SITES

Beast of Bray Road

http://www.beastofbrayroad.com

The author's continuing updates on contemporary sightings of werewolf-like creatures, particularly in the United States and Canada.
Also contains a page on the creature's history, a blog, an FAQ page,
as well as readers' comments.

Cryptozoology.com

http://www.cryptozoology.com

A Web site dedicated to the study of unknown animals presumed to be
physical, natural creatures. Contains breaking news stories, blogs,
and extensive forums.

The Malleus Maleficarum

http://urbanlegends.about.com/gi/dynamic/offsite.htm?zi=1/XJ&sdn
=urbanlegends&zu=http%3A%2F%2Fwww.malleusmaleficarum
.org%2F

Read the entire original text of *The Witch Hammer*, Papal Bull of Innocent VIII, with search capability.

The Mystic's Menagerie **on the Mystical World Wide Web**

http://www.mystical-www.co.uk/monster.html

A collection of descriptions of creatures either considered mythical or
with "mystic" connections, from the well-known to such obscure

entities as the "questing beast," said to sport the head of a snake, a leopard's body, and deer hooves.

The Werewolf Café

http://www.werewolfcafe.com

Werewolf art, stories, and forums at a site only open for the 36 hours surrounding each month's full moon. Splash page tells you when the next one will occur.

Werewolf—Wikipedia, the Free Encyclopedia

http://en.wikipedia.org/wiki/Werewolf

An overview of the werewolf throughout history, with several external links provided and some early European representations.

Wolf History—Canis dirus

http://www.naturalworlds.org/wolf/history/Canis_dirus.htm

A factual history of the dire wolf as well as other extinct and living wild canines.

PRINT

Frost, Brian J. *The Essential Guide to Werewolf Literature*. Madison, Wisc.: University of Wisconsin Press, 2003.

More than just a list of werewolf-related reference, nonfiction, and literature published before 2003, Frost also discusses and analyzes many of the more important works. It includes a segment on "Werewolf Stories for Children," noting titles, from R.L. Stine's *Goosebumps* series to Gordon Snell's *Curse of Werewolf Castle*.

Godfrey, Linda S. *The Beast of Bray Road: Tailing Wisconsin's Werewolf*. Madison, Wisc.: Prairie Oak Press (Trails Books), 2003.

The author's chronicle of how the 1990s Wisconsin werewolf flap known as The Beast of Bray Road sightings came about, including continued witness stories, historic context, possible explanations, and a chronology of events.

Godfrey, Linda S. *Hunting the American Werewolf.* Madison, Wisc.: Prairie Oak Press (Trails Books), 2006.

The author's continued exploration of many more contemporary sightings of furry, upright creatures not just in Wisconsin but across the U.S., with more history, added theories, Native American connections, and an expanded timeline.

Guiley, Rosemary Ellen. *The Encyclopedia of Vampires, Werewolves, and Other Monsters.* New York: Checkmark Books, 2004.

A comprehensive reference work for werewolves as well as their "kissing cousins," the vampires, and other related creatures. Includes literature, authors, legends, and terms. A particularly great source for synopses of vampire and werewolf films and novels, and for creatures of other cultures.

Steiger, Brad. *The Werewolf Book: The Encyclopedia of Shape-Shifting Beings.* Farmington Hills, Mich.: Visible Ink Press, 1999.

Devoted to all things remotely werewolfish, from obscure Portuguese shape-shifters called Bruxsa to examinations of serial killers such as Charles Manson. It includes an extensive chronology, and the Werewolf Resources appendix lists Web sites, fiction, nonfiction, and films (with synopses).

OTHER MEDIA

In Search of History: Legends of the Werewolves
History Channel DVD, April 2006

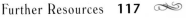

A 50-minute recap of the werewolf's tracks through time, starting with ancient Greece. Available from the History Channel Web site store. It includes an interview with author Gary Brandner, writer of *The Howling*.

Underworld (2003)
Underworld: Evolution (2006)
Sony Pictures, DVD

Two films that take a dark but entertaining look at an imaginary world where vampires and werewolves (called Lycans) in streetwise, tattered clothing battle out their ancient animosities on location in Budapest, Hungary. These contemporary "monster" movies add their own mythos to the traditional legends.

Werewolf: the Forsaken
White Wolf Publishing, 2005

A fantasy role-playing, Gothic horror-style game book featuring a race of werewolves who tread the area between the shadow world and the physical. It features five tribes of werewolves, its own creation legend, and opportunities for interacting with other types of magical beings.

Wolf
Sanctuary Woods, 1994

An older computer "game" for PC, still available from online sources—a remarkable true-to-life, role-playing simulation of the life of an actual wolf. It's not a game in the traditional sense, but provides what is probably the closest experience any human being can have of what it is like to be a wolf in the wild. Additional educational materials are included.

Bibliography

Aylesworth, G. Thomas. *Werewolves and other Monsters*. Reading, Mass.: Addison-Wesley Publishing Co., Inc., 1971.

Baring-Gould, Sabine. *The Book of Werewolves*. London, England: Senate, 1995 (orig. published 1865).

Bierhorst, John. *The Mythology of North America*. New York: Oxford University Press, 2002.

Birmingham, Robert A., and Leslie E. Eisenberg. *Indian Mounds of Wisconsin*. Madison, Wisc.: University of Wisconsin Press, 2000.

Boese, Alex. *Museum of Hoaxes: A Collection of Pranks, Stunts, Deceptions and Other Wonderful Stories Contrived for the Public from the Middle Ages to the New Millennium*. New York: Dutton, 2002.

Bueler, Lois. *Wild Dogs of the World*. New York: Stein and Day, 1973.

Dale-Green, Patricia. *Lore of the Dog*. Boston, Mass.: Houghton Mifflin, 1967.

Devereux, Paul. *Haunted Land: Investigations into Ancient Mysteries and Modern Day Phenomena*. London, England: Piatkus Books, 2001.

Dorf, Michael C. "How Reliable is Witness Testimony?" Findlaw for Legal Professionals. Available online. URL: http://writ.news.findlaw.com/dorf/20010516.html. Posted on May 16, 2001.

Douglas, Adam. *The Beast Within: A History of the Werewolf*. New York: Avon Books, 1992.

Edwards, Kathryn A., ed. *Werewolves, Witches and Wandering Spirits: Traditional Beliefs and Folklore in Early Modern Europe*. Kirksville, Miss.: Truman State University Press, 2002.

Evans, Bergen. *The Natural History of Nonsense*. New York: Alfred A. Knopf, Inc., 1971.

Fiske, John. "Werewolves and Swan-Maidens," *The Atlantic Monthly* 28 (August 1871).

Frost, Brian J. *The Essential Guide to Werewolf Literature.* Madison, Wisc.: University of Wisconsin Press, 2003.

Gill, Sam D., and Irene E. Sullivan. *Dictionary of Native American Mythology.* New York: Oxford University Press, 1992.

Godfrey, Linda S. *The Beast of Bray Road Home Page.* Available online. URL: http://www.beastofbrayroad.com. Updated August 23, 2006.

Godfrey, Linda S. *The Beast of Bray Road: Tailing Wisconsin's Werewolf.* Black Earth, Wisc.: Prairie Oak Press (Trails Books), 2003.

Godfrey, Linda S. *Hunting the American Werewolf.* Madison, Wisc.: Prairie Oak Press (Trails Books), 2006.

Greer, John Michael. *Monster: An Investigator's Guide to Magical Beings.* St. Paul, Minn.: Llewellyn Publications, 2002.

Guiley, Rosemary Ellen. *The Encyclopedia of Vampires, Werewolves, and Other Monsters.* New York: Checkmark Books, 2005.

Hall, Jamie. *Half Human, Half Animal: Tales of Werewolves and Related Creatures.* Bloomington, Ind.: Authorhouse (privately published), 2003.

Humphries, Ralph, trans. *Ovid: Metamorphoses.* Bloomington, Ind. and London, England: Indiana University Press, 1955.

Keel, John A. *The Complete Guide to Mysterious Beings.* New York: Tor Books, 2002.

Knappert, Jan. *Pacific Mythology: An Encyclopedia of Myth and Legend.* London, England: Diamond Books, 1995.

Lyons, Linda. "Paranormal Beliefs Come (Super)Naturally to Some," *Gallup Poll.* Available online. URL: http://poll.gallup.com/content/default.aspx?ci=19558&VERSION=p. Posted on November 1, 2005.

McCrady, Ellen. *The Ergot Epidemic* in *Mold Reporter,* from *Mold in Human History,* originally published as part of "Mold: The Whole Picture, Pt. 1," *Abbey Newsletter* 23 #4. Available online. URL: http://www.moldreporter.org/vol1no6/moldHist. Posted in 1999.

Morse-Kahn, Deborah. *A Guide to the Archaeology Parks of the Upper Midwest.* Lanham, Md.: Roberts Rinehart, 2003.

Munch, Peter Andreas. Revised by Magnus Olsen. Translated by Sigurd Bernhard Hustvedt. *Norse Mythology: Legends of Gods and Heroes.* New York: The American Scandinavian Foundation, 1963.

Mystical Worldwide Web. "Wolf," *The Mystic's Menagerie.* Available online. URL: http://www.mystical-www.co.uk/animal/animalw.htm#WOL. Downloaded on January 17, 2007.

O'Donnell, Elliott. *Werewolves.* Whitefish, Mont.: Kessinger Publishing, 2003.

Rein-Hagen, Mark. *Werewolf: The Apocalypse*, *Second Edition*: Stone Mountain, Calif.: White Wolf Game Studio, 1994.

Riggs, Robb. *In the Big Thicket: On the Trail of the Wild Man.* New York: Paraview Press, 2001.

Sanderson, Ivan. "The Missing Link," *Argosy* (May 1969): 23–31.

Schoolcraft, Henry R. *The Hiawatha Legends: North American Indian Lore.* Gwinn, Mich.: Avery Color Studios, 2001.

Slemens, Tom. *The Haunted Liverpool.* Liverpool, England: The Bluecoat Press, 2006.

Steiger, Brad. *The Werewolf Book: The Encyclopedia of Shape-Shifting Beings.* Farmington Hills, Mich.: Visible Ink Press, 1999.

Stringfellow, Jude. *Faith the Biped Dog*, Available online. URL: http://www .faiththedog.net. Updated January 14, 2007.

Summers, Montague. *The Werewolf in Lore and Legend.* Mineola, N.Y.: Dover Publications, 2003.

Trevor-Roper, H.R. *The European Witch Craze of the 16th and 17th Centuries and Other Essays.* New York: Harper and Row, 1967.

Walks-as-Bear, David. "Bear's Den," *The White Lake Beacon* (Whitehall, Mich., November 6, 2005.

Wolf, Fred Alan. *The Eagle's Quest: A Physicist's Search for Truth in the Heart of the Shamanic World.* New York: Summit Books, 1991.

Wolf History. "Canis dirus – Dire wolf," Available online. URL: http://www .naturalworlds.org/wolf/history/Canis_dirus.htm. Downloaded on January 17, 2007.

Woodward, Ian. *The Werewolf Delusion.* New York: Paddington Press, 1979.

Zenko, Darren. *Werewolves and Shapeshifters.* Auburn, Wash.: Ghost House Books (Lone Pine Publishing), 2004.

Index

A

"Abominable Snowman," 69
African folklore, 28
Algonquian folklore, 27
Allahabad, India, 50
Altered Beast (video game), 90
American Anthropological Research Foundation, 65
American Indian folklore. *See* Native American folklore
anecdotal evidence, 59, 107
animal skins, use of, 34–35
Anniston Star (newspaper), 71
Antarctic Press, 92
Anubis, 34, 103
Apollo, 38, 104
Argosy (magazine), 68
Asia Minor, 34
Atlantic Monthly, 59
Aurora, Minnesota, 69
Avon Bottoms wildlife refuge, 17, 106

B

Baldur's Gate II (video game), 90
The Beast of Bray Road (film), 44
The Beast of Bray Road: Tailing Wisconsin's Werewolf (Godfrey), 44
The Beast Within (Douglas), 33–34
The Beast Within (video game), 90
Belgian Royal Academy of Sciences, 69
Benedictbeuern, Germany, 61
Berber folklore, 28

berserkers, 34–35, 107
Bigfoot, 22, 44–45, 62, 63, 65, 107
Bigfoot tracks, 80–81
Big Thicket National Preserve, Texas, 61
biped, 76–77, 107
bipedal behavior of quadrupeds, 77
black "panthers," 61
Bluff Creek, California, 63, 64
booger (swamp monster), 72
books, on werewolves, 87
boudas, 28, 107
Bray Road, beast of, 41–45, 67–70
British folklore, 60
Bueler, Lois, 50
Buffy the Vampire Slayer (TV series), 87

C

Calcutta, India, 49
Calhoun County, Alabama, 71
canid, 77, 107
Catal Huyuk, 34, 103
Cerberus, 60
Chaney, Lon, Jr., 15, 84, 88–89
Charlemagne, 37
Cheyenne Dog Soldiers, 59, 104
Chichweya, 28, 107
Chimera: The Werewolf Cult Chronicles (film), 87
Choccolocco Monster, 71, 105
Christianity, 38–39
Cleveland Plain Dealer, 70–71
comic books, 91–92

Comics Code (1954), 91
congenital hypertrichosis, 51–53, 107
Constantinople, 38, 104
coyote, 22
Creamer, Michael, 71–72
cryptids, 98, 107
cryptozoologists, 22, 107
cults, 38, 104
Curse of the Were-Rabbit (animated film), 86–87

D

della Porta, Giambattista, 56
Devereux, Paul, 65
digitigrade footprints, 80, 107
dire wolf *(Canis dirus)*, 21, 103
DNA analysis, 73
dog man, 20, 81, 107. *See also* Michigan Dog Man
Dog Soldiers (film), 85
Dorf, Michael, 72
Douglas, Adam, 33–34

E

The Eagle's Quest (Wolf), 15
Eau Claire, Wisconsin, 75–76, 106
Edwards, Kathryn A., 15, 35
effigy mounds, 46–48, 103
Egyptian beliefs, 34, 103
electromagnetic (EM) force, 65, 101
The Encyclopedia of Vampires, Werewolves, and Other Monsters (Guiley), 53
ergot, 54–56, 108
The Essential Guide to Werewolf Literature (Frost), 87
Eternity, 91–92
etheric energy, 108
Europe, 27–28
European folklore, 35
excarnation, 34, 108

eyewitness accounts, unreliability of, 72–74

F

Faelad, 35
Faith (dog), 77–79, 105
FaiththeDog.net (Web site), 79
fauna, local, 97
feral children, 49–51, 104, 108
field gear, werewolf hunting, 97–98
footprints, 22
Fox, Michael J., 85
foxes, 28
France, 39
Fritz, Renee, 59
Frost, Brian J., 87

G

Gaboriaut, Jeanne, 32
Galen (Greek physician), 53
Gallup Poll, 12
Garm, 60
German immigrants, 39
Germany, 60–61
GetGhostGear.com (Web site), 100
Ginger Snaps (movies), 86
Gipson, Doris, 41–42, 105
Gold Digger (comic book), 92
Grateful Dead, 21
Great Bear Indian mound, 47
Greece, 38
Greek mythology, 60
Green Bay, Wisconsin, 39
Greer, John Michael, 101
Grenier, Jean, 31–34, 104
Guiley, Rosemary Ellen, 53

H

habitat, werewolf, 96
hair, on humans, 51–53

"Hairboy," 51
hallucinogens, 56
Hansen, Frank, 68, 105
"hard" evidence, 73
Harry Potter and the Prisoner of Azkaban
    (film), 87
Harry Potter and the Sorcerer's Stone
    (Rowling), 60
Haunted Land (Devereux), 65
The Haunted Liverpool (Slemen), 13
The Haunt of Fear (comic book), 91
hellhounds, 60–61
Heuvelmans, Bernard, 69
history, 31–39
hoaxes, 67–74
Ho-Chunk Indians, 46–48
Holy Roman Empire, 37
"Hound of Hell," 60
The Howling (film), 85
"How Reliable is Eyewitness Testi-
    mony?" (Dorf), 72
humans
    raised by wolves, 49–51
    resemblance to werewolves,
        49–56
    werewolf-like hair, 51–53
hunting, for werewolves, 93–102
Hunting the American Werewolf (Fritz),
    59–61
hyenas, 28, 70–71
hypertrichosis, 53

I

Ice Age, 22
India, 49–50, 104
Indian Mounds Park, 47
Innocent VIII (pope), 37, 103
Inquisition, 37–38
Inside Edition, 79
In the Big Thicket: On the Trail of the
    Wild Man (Riggs), 62

Irish folklore, 35
I Was a Teenage Werewolf (film), 85

J

jackal-headed god, 34
Japanese folklore, 28, 29

K

Keel, John, 61
Kelpies, 66
King, Stephen, 86
kitsune, 29, 108
Knight, Gabriel, 90
Kuala Lumpur, Malaysia, 29–30

L

La Brea tar pits, 21
La Loba (Wolf Woman), 14
Landon, Michael, 85
legends, 39
Lima Marsh wildlife refuge, 93
literature, on werewolves, 87
loup-garou, 27, 39, 108
LSD, 55
lycanthrope, 20, 108
lycanthropy, 35, 53, 108
Lycaon (Greek king), 20, 53

M

Magiae Naturalis (Natural Magic), 56
magicians, 22, 108
Maiolo, Bishop, 36
Malaysian folklore, 29–30
Malleus Maleficarum ("The Witch's
    Hammer"), 37, 103
man/animal connections, 34–35
man wolf, 20, 108
Marvel Comics, 91
megafauna, 45, 108
Menominee folklore, 27

mental disorders, 20, 53
metempsychosis, 59–60, 108
Michigan Dog Man, 13–14, 44, 104–106
Middle Ages, 12–13
Minnesota Ice Man, 68–69, 105
"miracle book," 60–61
Mitsumine, 28
Mokwayo, 27
Monsters (Greer), 101
Montel Williams Show, 77
movies, werewolves in, 83–90
Munch, Peter Andreas, 35
mystery cats, 61
The Mystic's Menagerie (Web site), 11

N
Native American folklore, 58–59. *See also folklore of specific tribes, e.g.:* Algonquian folklore
Navajo Indians, 22, 85
Nelson, Kevin, 95, 98
New Orleans, Louisiana, 39
New World, werewolf legends in, 39
Nigeria, 28, 104
Norse folklore/mythology, 34–35, 60
Norse Mythology (Munch), 35
North Wales, 13, 104

O
Oaxaca, Mexico, 14
O'Donnell, Elliott, 11
Ojibwe Indians, 25–26, 46
Oprah, 79

P
paranormal phenomena, 101
Parks, Nick, 86–87
Patterson, Roger, 63
Paulding County, Ohio, 70, 104

Paulding Light, 62
phantom dogs, 60–61
phantom wolves, 60–61
plantigrade footprints, 80, 108
plaster of Paris, 100
Pleistocene, 21
Poirier, Marguerite, 31
Pont-Saint-Esprit, France, 54, 105
porphyria, 52, 108
Potawatomi Indians, 46
public opinion polls, 12

Q
quadrupeds, 76–77, 109

R
Ragnarok, 60
Ramos-Gomez, Gabriel and Victor, 51
Reed City, Michigan, 14
Rein-Hagen, Mark, 90
religion, 34
Riggs, Robb, 62
Rock County, Wisconsin, 17, 93
role-playing games, 87, 90
Romulus and Remus, 50
Rowling, J. K., 60
Russia, 36

S
St. Anthony's Fire, 55
St. Patrick, 35, 103
Sanderson, Ivan T., 68
santu sakai, 29–30, 105, 109
Sasquatch. *See* Bigfoot
Scotland, 66
searching, for werewolves, 93–102
Serbia, 38
shamans, 22, 109
shape-shifter, 20, 22, 58–59, 85, 109
Sharon, Wisconsin, 59–60

Shawnee Nation, 58
Sheboygan, Wisconsin, 47
shrine of Saint Anastasia, 61
Siberia, 36–38
sightings
Eau Claire, Wisconsin, 75–76
Elkhorn, Wisconsin, 41–45
northern New York, 44
North Wales, 13
Rock County, Wisconsin, 93
Sharon, Wisconsin, 59–60
southern Georgia, 44
Wisconsin, 17–18
Sikandra, India, 50
Silver Bullet (film), 86
Singh, Joseph Amrito Lal, 49, 51
Siodmak, Curtis, 84–85
skinchanger, 22
skinwalker, 20, 22
Slemen, Tom, 13
Snorri Sturluson, 35, 103
"Snout-Nose," 65
Solyman II (Ottoman emperor), 38, 104
Spider-man (comic book series), 91
spirit messengers, 34
spirits, 45, 57–66
Stone Age hunting societies, 34
Stringfellow, Laura, 78
Stringfellow, Reuben and Jude, 79
sumangat, 30, 109
Summers, Montague, 32, 35, 36, 39
Summit Springs, Battle of, 59
Superior, Wisconsin, 71
Sweden, 35

T

Tales from the Crypt (comic book), 91
Teen Wolf (film), 85
telepathy, 59–60, 109
therianthropy, 109

Timor folklore, 30
tools, for werewolf searchers, 98–102
Traverse City, Michigan, 44
trials, 37–38
trifield meter, 101

U

Underworld (film), 86
Underworld: Evolution (film), 86
Universal Pictures, 84
Upper Peninsula, Michigan, 62

V

vampires, 38
Van Dyke, Richard, 65
Van Helsing (film), 84, 85
vargr, 35, 109
The Vault of Horror (comic book), 91
video games, 87, 90
Voss, Noah, 95, 98, 100
voukoudlaks, 38, 109

W

waarwolf, 39, 109
Wales, 13, 104
Walks-As-Bear, David, 58–59
Walworth County, 42
The Werewolf (film), 85, 104
Werewolf at Large (comic book), 91–92
Werewolf by Night (comic book), 91
The Werewolf in Lore and Legend (Summers), 32
Werewolf of London (film), 85
Werewolf: The Apocalypse (game), 90
Werewolves (O'Donnell), 11
Werewolves, Witches and Wandering Spirits (Edwards), 35
Wild Dogs of the World (Bueler), 50
Williamson, Neal, 71–72
"window" areas, 61

Wisconsin, 46–48, 104
witch trials, 37–38, 104
With a Little Faith (Stringfellow), 79
Wolf, Fred Alan, 14–15
"Wolf Brothers," 51
Wolf Lake (TV series), 87
Wolf Man (Siodmak), 84
The Wolf Man (film), 84
"wolves' fury," 53

Y

Yakuts folklore, 36–38
yenaldlooshi, 22, 109
YouTube.com (Web site), 77
Yu Zhenhuan, 51, 52

Z

Zahn, Katie, 17–19, 106
Zeus, 38, 104

About the Author

LINDA S. GODFREY worked as a newspaper reporter and columnist for *The Week*, a county newspaper published in Delavan, Wisconsin, for 10 years. She won National Newspaper Association first-place awards for feature stories in 1996, 1998, and 2000. She is the author of *The Beast of Bray Road* and *Hunting the American Werewolf*, as well as two volumes in the Barnes & Noble "Weird" series: *Weird Wisconsin* (co-authored with Richard D. Hendricks) and *Weird Michigan*. She has appeared on many national television and radio programs as an expert on anomalous creatures, including *Inside Edition*, Animal Planet Channel, *The New In Search Of* (SCI FI Channel), Travel Channel, Discovery Kids, *Northern Mysteries* on Canada's Global Network, and the *Jeff Rense*, *Clyde Lewis*, *Rob McConnell*, and *Coast to Coast AM* radio shows. She is also an illustrator and artist, and she maintains a Web site on werewolf sightings and news at www.beastofbrayroad.com. She lives with her husband, Steven, in rural southeastern Wisconsin.

About the Consulting Editor

ROSEMARY ELLEN GUILEY is one of the foremost authorities on the paranormal. Psychic experiences in childhood led to her lifelong study and research of paranormal mysteries. A journalist by training, she has worked full time in the paranormal since 1983, as an author, presenter, and investigator. She has written 31 nonfiction books on paranormal topics, translated into 13 languages, and hundreds of articles. She has experienced many of the phenomena she has researched. She has appeared on numerous television, documentary, and radio shows. She is also a member of the League of Paranormal Gentlemen for Spooked Productions, a columnist for *TAPS Paramagazine*, a consulting editor for *FATE* magazine, and writer for the "Paranormal Insider" blog. Ms. Guiley's books include *The Encyclopedia of Angels*, *The Encyclopedia of Magic and Alchemy*, *The Encyclopedia of Saints*, *The Encyclopedia of Vampires, Werewolves, and Other Monsters*, and *The Encyclopedia of Witches and Witchcraft*, all from Facts On File. She lives in Maryland and her Web site is http://www.visionaryliving.com.